Baldwins

OMEGA

The First 30 Years

An Introduction: Baldwin's Omega
The First 30 Years

Baldwin's Omega has been an all-absorbing passion for me and my family for 30 years. And long may it continue. This book was intended to be a loose record of those three decades, one I hope you enjoy in that context and find informative, entertaining and sometimes quite amusing.

It's not an easy task to recall all the people and events who have helped make the place what it is today, so apologies if I've missed anyone out. Don't take it personally.

So where did it all start? You could say with a vision. My dream was to give Sheffield a place where diners could expect, and consistently find, fine food for whatever number of guests were in the room at the time. I hope we've achieved that, but whatever happens we will continue to strive for perfection. You never know, we may get there someday.

Seriously, I do hope you enjoy the book, even if it's not to be taken too seriously. And if you are one of those missed out, take heart. We are now compiling stories for the second book so please feel free to email me at david@baldwinsomega.com.

May I wish you a life of good food, great wine and lots of friends.

Sincerely yours,

Big 'Un

Foreword by Brian Turner CBE

No matter how long you think you've known David Baldwin or the 'Big Un' as he is known to us cooks it seems like you've known him forever. In his part of the world some say – "them he doesn't know, isn't worth knowing and them that doesn't know the Omega, knows 'nowt about eating." David Baldwin is the Omega and the Omega is David Baldwin, not forgetting of course the 'Little Un', his loyal principal supporter and main stay, his wife the delicious Pauline.

I have to admit I haven't been to Baldwin's Omega as often as I would like but whenever I have been, I have just loved the honesty, simplicity and the welcome, of the people, the place and the food. The 'Big 'Un' is a man who has invested in the future of many of his staff by just sending them off to work with people he looks up to. They have all gone back to the Omega and put something back into the business, and it shows.

Wherever Baldwin and his team go they are anxious to learn and to bring back this learning to the institution that is Baldwin's Omega. However for me to sum up Baldwin's I have to use the word that I think is not understood by enough people in our industry today and that word is 'Hospitality'. Baldwin's is all about hospitality, the dictionary says this means – the friendly and liberal reception of guest and strangers, at Baldwin's Omega the welcome is more than friendly, its positively heart warming. You never want to leave and most times I've been there I don't remember leaving!

David Baldwin and Baldwin's Omega bring to this world of ours a great example of what hospitality is all about, long may it continue.

Anyone who greets me from across a crowded room in London and shouts 'y'all reet love?' has to be my kind of man. It's a privilege to call him my dear friend David Baldwin.

Brian Turner CBE

Acknowledgements

Dedicated to the memory of the late **Ted Horsewood**
Gentleman, dear friend, great supporter and an inspiration,
who always believed in the Omega dream.
Thanks Ted.

Sincere thanks to all our long serving or should it be enduring staff.
Especially **Janet Wilson, Stephen Roebuck, Ian Roberts, Sam Lindsay,
Joan Osguthorpe, Angela Jackson, Mary Hazleton, Jamie Christian,
Sam Sanderson, Jeni Morley, Jean Percival**
and many more, thank you, thank you, thank you.

To all our many ex-staff who have passed through our doors,
many on their way to illustrious careers and others
who have just stayed with us until retirement.
**Roy Barson, Bernard Strutt, Anne & Les White, John Simpson,
Mary Booker, Raymond Booker, Pamela Corkell, Jeremy Plester**
To name but a few.

To our friends **Gian Bohan** & **Maurizio Mori** at Nonna's
whose beautiful book inspired us to write this one.

Brian Turner CBE – Our good friend and mentor.

Gordon Clark – For a great 17 years!

Dr. Dick Atkinson
Thanks for our train journey and the poetic results, just great.

Martin Edwards, **Paul Cocker** and all the staff at RMC Books.

Polly A. Baldwin, our daughter without whom the book would never have been
published, thanks for the wonderful photographs and all your hard work.

My friends, **Mark Rodgers** & **Martin Dawes** at Sheffield Newspapers
for their unstinting support and archive material, so freely given.

Very special thanks to all our supporters,
we hope you have enjoyed the first thirty years as much as we have
and look forward to many more.

David & Pauline Baldwin

Written by:
© David & Pauline Baldwin
Baldwin's Omega Ltd
Brincliffe Hill, Off Psalter Lane
Sheffield S11 9DF
Telephone: (0114) 255 1818
www.baldwinsomega.com

Photography, except where mentioned:
© Polly A. Baldwin
www.dynamicpictures.co.uk

Edited by:
Martin Edwards, Chris Brierley
RMC Books – (0114) 250 6300

Design by:
Paul Cocker
RMC Books – (0114) 250 6300

Contributors:
Andy Waple, Trevor Wright, Gordon Clark,
Polly A. Baldwin, Ben Baldwin,
Angus & Oscar Baldwin, David Baldwin Jr,
Martin Dawes & Sheffield Newspapers Ltd,
Frances Soar, Mary Wilkinson,
Thomas Robinson, Audrey Hobson,
Alice Potter

First Published in 2010 on behalf of:
Baldwin's Omega Ltd. – www.baldwinsomega.com

Published by:
RMC Books – www.rmcbooks.co.uk

Contents

Ode to Baldwin's

From the cruise ships via the Anglers Rest
Baldwin's Omega has become the ultimate test.
Restaurateur, bon viveur, auctioneer,
Pauline is Madame and David the Monsieur.

Where in Sheffield for your special function?
A wedding, a dinner, that special luncheon;
There's only one place, it's on Psalter Lane
A standard of catering only Baldwin's can attain.

Be it Golf Club dinner or Pony Club ball
Baldwin's has the staff to cater for all.
A late bar and disco, the dance floor heaving
Whether dinner jacket or casual for that special evening.

Fillet de boeuf or pudding crème anglaise
David's the expert on a menu in Franglais
Salmon and Strawberries or Caribbean Parties
None of your fancy food and café lattes.

Tuesday to Friday enjoy the 'plat du jour'
Just ring Sam's office 'certainly a table for four'
It used to be business lunches then ordering more rounds
A lot of them now are blue rinse and grey pounds.

Where but the Omega a classic Italian Risotto?
Whilst 'fun in a bun' is the young proms motto.
'Try it you'll like it', specially Granny Baldwin's tart
Then follow with Stilton and its cousins from Montmartre.

A lady one day ordered wild roast pheasant
And complained to the staff in a manner not pleasant
'Mr Baldwin' she said 'there's shot in my meat'
'Does tha' think it had heart attack and died at my feet?'

New Year '87 was part French, part British
The Tunnel announced so a menu quite skittish
Payment 30 in pounds or by francs was the deal
Champagne, left bank stompers and a seven course meal.

Sports personalities and Ladies' Lunch with fashion
All cooking and presentation is done with passion
There's Campillo and Faustino wine tasting with dinner
We all eat six courses and get no thinner.

There's Motown revival and Ascot Ladies' nights
April in Paris and Christmas parties with lights
Smokey R's chicken presented with flares
Then Summer Cup over 2 miles for the lady stayers.

German, Austrian, French and New World
A balanced wine list in front of you unfurled,
House specials are mixed by David on tour
Tempranillo, Sauvignon, Grenache, perhaps a touch more.

Each one of their guests will have had good fare
Weddings, birthdays, funerals, all take us there
As the years roll past, too many meals to mention
We all agree 'your special occasion deserves our attention'

Ready for a change, banks of new lights,
Alpha and rib rooms give us some new sights.
But what can you do to upgrade the gents?
Make it 'Loo of the Year' and add some new scents!

In such busy lives celebrations abound,
First forty, then fifty and seventy came round;
Each with feasts presided over by mine host
And appreciated by us punters, their health to toast.

Not many restaurants keep such loyal staff
Janet's been long enough to wear her own path
Steve the head chef there man and boy
Jamie and Angela also long in employ.

Keith Floyd, Raymond Blanc, the Brothers Roux
Big David's friends read like a catering 'who's who'
As Restaurant Society Chairman he's been everywhere
Now to present an honour with pride we all share.

How do you reward a couple so hearty?
From Buck Palace came an invite to the garden party
Shiny shoes, bib and tucker, scone and jam
"We're from north o't Wash, come and join us Ma'am".

So 30 years on what does the future hold?
For David and Pauline who refurbish so bold
Is there anything else to which the Baldwin's aspiring?
A secret at present because he's **"not f***ing retiring".**

Written by: Dr Dick Atkinson, medical friend and proud patron of Baldwin's Omega.

200 Years BB (Before Baldwin)

The Story of Brincliffe Hall

It is said the land at Brincliffe was once the hunting ground for the noblemen of Hassop and Chatsworth. Certainly, Sheffield archives have documents dating back to the 1700s that would seem to support this. For those who find it hard to imagine toffs on horseback galloping down Chelsea Road in pursuit of the local wildlife, we should think of the area as the wooded pasture it once was. To help us, we have at least one window into the past. The earliest record we have of the area our restaurant occupies is this painting by Sheffield artist JW McIntyre entitled 'A View of Sheffield from Psalter Lane' painted about 1850. The quarry face which is the main image of the picture is still to be seen in our car park today. The quarry was one of many in the area excavating the precious sandstone for building houses and, crucially, for the grinding wheels that helped to make Sheffield's steel industry so successful.

The Brincliffe quarries were eventually abandoned, many being partially filled in and used for building land. Ours met the same fate in the late 19th century, with the result that the original quarry floor is twenty to thirty feet below the area now occupied by our car park.

Where the present building stands once stood Brincliffe Hall. Legend has it this was an impressive building but sadly the only evidence of it today, apart from old maps, are remnants of the old rose garden which can still be seen from our kitchen window round the back of the building.

It is not clear when our building first appeared but it is known that it stood alongside Brincliffe Hall for many years. In the early part of the 20th century the two became a tennis and social club. The tennis courts covered the area where our car park stands now. Spectators could take in all the centre court action from our Rib Room, which was in those days a grand viewing terrace. The club was hired out in the same way as a modern day community centre. Over the years we have had many customers who remember this time with immense fondness. Regrettably I can't recall all of the accounts in detail but here is one lovely memory of the hall being used for dancing just before the war, from Frances Soar and her mother, Mary Soar nee Wilkinson.

'My mother, now in her late eighties, tells me that she has a very soft spot for Brincliffe Hall and spent some of the most happy times of her life there. She recalls that when she was in her early teens (in the mid 1930s) she started going to Miss Isobel Lockwood's ballroom dancing classes on Psalter Lane.

It was more of a dance club really. We learned a few steps, then just danced! After the end of term, when we felt we could progress to real dances, we (by this time we were quite a little group) started going to Brincliffe Hall. I remember particularly the 'flannel dances' held in the summer. None of us belonged to the tennis club but I think the club organised the dances. The tickets were about 2/6d; I can't remember whether that included refreshments. There was a proper dance band I think Albert Hunter was a regular. Our little group used to gather in a small room at the end of the ballroom. When I was sixteen I was working at a firm of Chartered Accountants and they hired the hall for their annual staff party. There was no alcohol, but we didn't miss it – we just enjoyed dancing. This lovely time came to an end when the Second War started and we all went our different ways"

There must be a lot of friendly ghosts at the Omega!'

Frances Soar

The Hall was also used by the Bluecoat School. Originally based in the city centre, the school also founded a new building on part of the old quarry site in 1911, using stone from our quarry. This building later became part of the Sheffield Hallam University Arts Centre, which at the time of writing was being converted into dwellings. Bluecoats was a charitable school that existed to provide education for young boys mainly from single-parent families and orphans whose fathers died during World War One. Ironically the school was disbanded in 1939 and the school building, along with Brincliffe Hall, was requisitioned by the Army for use during World War Two. Our building formed part of the drill hall for the men who were stationed on the site at Psalter Lane during World War Two. There are a few eye-witness accounts of this time including this one from Thomas Robinson:

> *"The Brincliffe quarries were taken over by the Army in World War Two and I remember seeing the sentries at the top of the Psalter Hill. There were also rifle ranges there".*

We also know that an anti-aircraft battery was stationed here, probably due to its elevated position above the city. The site played a big part in the protection of Sheffield's vital steel industry throughout the war.

After the war Sheffield Corporation took over responsibility for the site. Part of it was developed into an education facility that later became Sheffield Arts College, and subsequently part of Sheffield Hallam University. Our part of the quarry site where the Brincliffe Hall tennis club still stood was eventually sold in the late 1950s to Sheffield Refreshment Houses Ltd. Already the owners of Sheffield's most popular hotels and restaurants, they were out to impress with this purchase. They wanted to open a new modern restaurant to rival the fancy restaurants in London. The city's heritage was to pay a high price because of this. Sadly the old hall was judged to be the wrong style and although it was a listed building, it was demolished and replaced with an extension to the our current building. The owners picked up an £800 fine for their trouble but it meant they could achieve their ultra-modernist ideals for the new restaurant.

The lounge and bar, a beautifully furnished room where customers may sit in comfort to drink cocktails and aperitifs while waiting to take their tables for dinner.

will be allowed to visit the kitchen if they wish.

Everything from that lump of ice in your drink to the scampi on the table is prepared to match the surrounding luxury.

And that lump of ice is special. It is produced by an ice-making machine, manufactured in Britain on an American idea.

REQUESTS
FOR BOOKINGS

The kitchen is tiled and designed for optimum hygiene. It has every desirable kitchen device and gives the chef plenty of space in which to work.

It is stocked up with top-

class cutlery and china which will feature on the tables with silverware to complete the picture.

Mr. Milne feels that the Omega will fill a great gap in Sheffield's night-life and facilities. Already he has been besieged by requests for bookings.

In every aspect of the Omega project he has tried to aim for perfection and he knows the high standard he has set.

The luxury is not superficial. It would have been easy enough to put in a few fake panelled walls but the wood of the Omega is real.

It would have been just as easy to have an elaborate restaurant with no

additional comforts even the deep-piled peted ladies' powder has that same finish.

At a time when all over the country losing their reserv savouring fully th sures of dining Omega seems to especially important

Mr. Milne is qu about its purposes kind of people attract. It is exp present provinci dards. An evening your wife, a busin or a girl friend leave much chan "fiver."

But for the will get at the Milne is sure th had value for

feature on the new restaurant is continued on Page 12.

feature on the new restaurant is continued on Page 12.

Omega

one of Sheffield's tom restaurants has closed its doors for the last some running a first-aid post round the clock site Reincliffe is to be used for housing.

It has not yet been decided whether the restaurant will be demolished or face a change of use.

Managing director of Chelsea of Sheffield, who own the Omega, Steve Hinchliffe, said: "We are closing the restaurant because the planning authorities have

Group sell restaurant in Sheffie

Morning Telegraph Reporter

Sheffield Refreshment Houses is sell its restaurants and concentrating on ho

It has sold the Omega and Kenwood R. Steve Hinchliffe, the chairman and mana Abbey Garage, for £170,000.

The money from the sale will be used to reduce the group's bank borrowing on two recent buys — Roslyn Court Hotel and St Andrew's Hotel, both in Sheffield Together they cost £500,000.

The other chairman, Mr C Edward Lowe and he did not other than sales and managing was to make a portfolio, but the sale would benefit the company's long-term strat

"We are concentrating on the hotel industry on rather than these restaurant and we have...

The Last Word in Sheffield Fine Dining

The year 1962 is chiefly remembered as the era of mop-top haircuts, The Beatles and the tense few days the world stood on the brink of nuclear war in the Cuban missile crisis. But even as JFK and Khrushchev were staring each other down, at least some of us were optimistic about what the future held.

The new restaurant opened in a blaze of glory. There was a genuine buzz of excitement throughout the city about its new modern British theme. The building had been constructed in the most up-to-date style and the interior was much talked about. The main dining room, now our Ballroom, boasted 140 covers surrounding one of the few sprung dance floors in Sheffield, which in turn was illuminated by a hanging ceiling of light, the first of its kind anywhere in the country. It also had a smaller dining room, still known as the 'Alpha room' for private dining, and a lounge bar, known to us now as the 'Long room' and still used for a similar purpose. The present day 'Rib room' was a later addition.

The name of the new restaurant reflected its cutting edge concept. Omega, the last letter of the Greek alphabet W, signified the ultimate, the last word in fine dining. It was a fitting name for a restaurant that set out to impress. And the newspapers back in September of that year were certainly captivated by the new arrival.

From the tone of the press coverage, the reader could be forgiven for thinking that opening night went off without a hitch. But Trevor Wright, the manager of the Omega, recalls it differently;

'It was September 1962, the actual day escapes me, but we were excited and ready for the big night. The previous night had been a trial run for staff, family members, contractors who had worked on the project and the local press.

It was a fixed menu with wine preceded by a free reception. It ran very smoothly and everyone had a good time and we received excellent comments including a very nice press review.

It was with this in mind that we looked forward to the official opening. The house was packed with the city's movers and shakers. Our restaurant staff mostly hired away from the Grand Hotel were ready and eager to please.

The kitchen brigade were completely new to Sheffield. I was told they were brought up from London, including the pearl divers (dishwashers) and they were all male. The head chef was a French Canadian who seemed to know his stuff, but confused the entire staff by giving the menu items numbers similar to a Chinese restaurant.

When the orders came into the kitchen, they were placed on the stainless steel counter top (at the time we did not have a table numbers pegboard) which was a big mistake. Then someone opened the outside kitchen door and a gust of wind scattered the orders like confetti! Needless to say, it threw the entire system into chaos. People who were ready for their main course had to wait another hour or so, people who had just ordered in the lounge were having their starters delivered before they were seated, the brave who sat it out finally received their meals around 1am!
I received over three dozen bottles of wine back that had been opened but not consumed because the food never came out.

One of the Directors who was on duty that night was totally embarrassed by the events, he gave me the keys and said, "Trevor, lock up!"

That turned out to be my job for the next 15 years...'

J. Trevor Wright

Trevor Wright, the first manager of the Omega
Reproduced with kind permission from Sheffield Newspapers Ltd.

LUXURY RESTAURANT OPENS

CIVIC ACCLAIM AS CITY'S NEW LUXURY RESTAURANT OPENS

Looks delicious. Nine-year-old Ann, daughter of Mr S. R. Milne, managing director Sheffield Refreshment Houses Ltd., is show the decorated boar's head at last night's dinner to mark the opening of Sheffield's new Omega Restaurant. With her are Mr. Henry Dixon, chairman, and chef Andy De Vine.

Gourmet's paradise 'will enhance Sheffield's tourist ambitions'

The two leading figures in the "Make Sheffield a tourist centre" campaign – the Lord Mayor, Ald. P. J. Kirkham and his deputy, Ald. James Sterland – got together yesterday. They were dining at the celebration opening of the Omega Restaurant – Sheffield's luxury new eating spot.

And Mr. Henry Dixon, chairman of Sheffield Refreshment Houses Limited, who own the new restaurant, revealed that it was the campaign by the Lord Mayor and Ald. Sterland which has clinched the idea of opening the new premises.

Said the Lord Mayor: "Our campaign is now being emphasised by people like yourselves. At last we have got some people interested in putting into practice what we have been after.

"This, I hope, will be only the first of many such establishments."

EXCELLENT

The new restaurant was of "the finest quality attainable" – an excellent thing for Sheffield, said the Lord Mayor.

Ald. Sterland said: "What we have to decide is what Sheffield has to offer the people who will be coming to the city from Europe and from further shores."

The new restaurant would be one thing to offer the visitors with pride, he said.

Mr. Dixon said that the Omega had not been built to be in competition with the Kenwood Hall – also owned by his company – but rather to supplement it.

Despite rumours to the contrary, he added, the Omega would not be a night club in the accepted sense of the term.

The luncheon, attended by more than 100 businessmen and some of the city's principal council members and officials, was followed in the evening by a dinner with another impressive guest list at which the civic guests were also present.

During the lunch gathering, the Lord Mayor unveiled a beautiful mural photograph of the Surprise View at Hathersage taken by Mr. Dick Mottershaw, managing director of Photo Finishers (Sheffield) Ltd.

The Deputy Lord Mayor unveiled a mural of the view from the restaurant at the top of Psalter Lane.

For the evening guests these ceremonies were repeated by two of the directors, Mr. Norman Harding and Mr. Bob Milne, managing director of Sheffield Refreshment Houses. The other directors, Mr. L. Lewis, the secretary, and Mr. S. H. Todd, were also present.

Today the restaurant is open to the public.

Sheffield's plush new Omega Restaurant, which claims to have the finest kitchens in the Provinces, is open to the public today.

Guests at a dinner to celebrate the opening saw two magnificent murals unveiled by Mr Bob Milne, managing director, and Mr Norman Harding, director of Sheffield Refreshment Houses Ltd., the restaurant's proprietors.

The twin ceremonies were a repeat of the unveilings earlier by the Lord Mayor, Ald. Percy Kirkman, and the Deputy Lord Mayor, Ald. J.W. Sterland.

MURALS

Depicted on the murals are the Surprise View at Hathersage and a view of the area around the restaurant in Psalter Lane as it was 100 years ago.

The Omega is a marvel of rapid reconstruction work.

Formerly known as Brincliffe Hall, it was bought by the Refreshment Houses in April and contractors began the work of transforming it into a luxurious modern restaurant only 20 weeks ago.

Now there is an elegant dining room with seating for 140 people around a small dance floor, a 60-seater dining room for small private parties and a sumptuous lounge.

PRAISE

Both the Lord Mayor and Deputy Lord Mayor have praised the idea behind the Omega as a means of helping Sheffield's drive to attract more visitors.

Directors of Sheffield Refreshment Houses Ltd. in addition to Mr. Milne and Mr Harding are Mr. Henry Dixon, chairman, Mr L. Lewis and Mr. S.H. Todd.

A montage of press cuttings over the years, these two from the opening of The Omega 20th September 1962
Reproduced with kind permission from Sheffield Newspapers Ltd.

Cooking up a route from rags to riches

By John Highfield

SHEFFIELD Culinary superstar David Baldwin owes his success – in the best rags to riches tradition – to the hardships of childhood.

The literally larger-than-life, straight-talking owner of the popular Baldwin's Omega function suite and restaurant looks back on 50 years which have taken him around the world and made him a South Yorkshire celebrity.

But he admits that things might have been different if his widowed mother had not had to go out to work to support her young family.

"I suppose I was one of the original latch-key kids" he laughs. "When you are hungry at four o'clock and your mum isn't coming home till six you learn how to cook very quickly.

"There was no fast food in those days either – I can remember the revolution in the 50s when a local chip shop started to open at tea time".

A Sheffield man, David was born and brought up in the Broomhall area and one of his favourite topics is the way in which the district was, in later years, to be destroyed by ambitious town planners.

"It is a planner's nightmare now" he claims. "I can never understand why planners are so smug when they have never got anything right."

SCIENCE

"They knocked all those lovely old terrace houses down when all they needed was a Grand or so spending on them at the time to get rid of the outside toilets."

All his childhood was spent at Springfield School – where domestic science was strictly for the girls.

Nevertheless, the call of the kitchen had already taken hold and, with school behind him, he took the first of many jobs, at Tuckwoods Restaurant in Surrey Street – "still the best restaurant in Sheffield because it serves proper food."

When a week-long holiday break went on for 21 days though, he was given the sack and a lifelong pattern of not being a long-serving member of anybody's staff was established.

"I was always totally impossible if I was in the same place for more than six months," he admits. "I suppose you could say I was a bit volatile – crazy was a word people often used – and it was a convenient way of changing jobs."

A similarly short-lived experience at the long-gone Grand Hotel – "that's where I discovered that, unlike most of the British population, I did enjoy giving service" – was followed by the first of life's major upheavals.

LEGENDARY

"You could call the Merchant Navy the university of life," he explains. "I joined that rather than doing National Service with the army or being a Bevin Boy".

"I only decided that I had seen enough of the world when I heard that they had stopped National Service."

His return to Sheffield saw him taking a short break from catering when he worked for legendary city market trader "Potty" Edwards.

That was followed by a period in the kitchens at Sheffield's Nether Edge, Firvale and City General before he took his first pub – the Central Tavern in Nottingham.

Just five years later, he was back in Sheffield, working at the Omega in Psalter Lane and little realising that he would eventually own it.

That was followed by a couple of years at another vanished city landmark, Hopkinson's Fish and Chip restaurant at the bottom of The Moor.

"It was possible around this time that I first started to think about settling down properly," he says. "I was there over two years which was a lifetime to me in terms of what I had done before."

FAMOUSLY

After running the Bee Hive in Hillsborough and tackling the Wheatsheaf in Ecclesall – "that was really a shop window for me" – things took off in a big way as he took over a string of pubs and restaurants, including the Anglers Rest at Bamford, the Prince of Wales at Baslow and – most famously – the Hillsborough Suite at the Sheffield Wednesday ground.

"This was my empire-building phase," he says. "The Hillsborough Suite was the most successful business I had ever had and, apart from where I am now, was the one I enjoyed the most."

In 1981 came the chance to return to the Omega – this time as owner and with his name over the door and, now almost a decade later, he seems finally to have set down permanent roots with wife Pauline and his three children, aged 13, 14 and 24.

IMPROVED

With so much accomplished, he can look back with pleasure on a career that has thrived without any formal training.

"Food is not just my job it has always been my life and I love it," he says.

In fact, he even blames college training for the move away from traditional cooking towards increasing stylisation in food preparation.

"Nouvelle Cuisine has been good in one way because it has generally improved the concept of food and lifted the expectations of the British," he says.

"Things move on, though and two or three years ago I re-named it Renaissance Cuisine – which means Nouvelle Cuisine but with a little bit more on the plate!"

Larger-than-life David Baldwin in his kitchen

'I suppose I was one of the original latch-key kids'

From Rags to Riches by John Highfield, 19th May 1990 in The Sheffield Star
Reproduced with kind permission from Sheffield Newspapers Ltd.

A new luxury restaurant opens tomorrow

A panoramic view of the main dining room, where luxury is the key word. Tables to seat 140 people are set out around a main dance floor. One of the most remarkable features is the hanging ceiling of laminated material – the only one of its kind in the country – which diffuses a warm light.

FOR A CLIENTELE PREPARED TO PAY FOR PERFECTION

By A Special Correspondent

SHEFFIELD as a tourist centre – a city with nightlife – or is this just wishful thinking?

The City's Lord Mayor, Ald. Jim Sterland, didn't think so and said so in no uncertain terms. The publicity that his idea brought planted a very firm idea in the minds of the directors of Sheffield Refreshment Houses Ltd, the owners of Kenwood Hall.

In April this year they bought Brincliffe Hall, just off Psalter Lane. Tomorrow it will open as possibly the most luxurious restaurant outside London.

The word "luxury" can sound like just another word out of the salesman's vocabulary, but for once any other description would be inappropriate.

In the last five months the interior of the old Hall has been ripped out, including the windows and inside walls. Around the shell has grown the "Omega."

In no part of the fitting, from the wallpaper to the kitchen and tableware, has expense been spared. At every turn the prime thought has been to cater for a clientele who want to dine out luxuriously and are prepared to pay for perfection.

Mr Bob Milne, the Managing Director, has toured England getting ideas for the new self-contained restaurant. He feels there is a real need for such an establishment in Sheffield for people who want to dine out well or entertain their business associates.

From the large car park and porch-canopy over the entrance every foot of the Omega has been tailored for the customer's benefit.

The highlight is of course the dining room, which will seat 140 people. The tables will be mounded around a small dance floor.

The ceiling is one of the most remarkable features, for it is a hanging ceiling of laminated material, the only one of its sort in the country. It spreads a warm diffused light throughout the room.

All the seats are leather-backed, and diners can make themselves comfortable any time between the times of 12.30 and 3 p.m. and 6.30 p.m. to 2 a.m., from Monday to Saturday and up to 11.30 p.m. on Sunday, during which times the restaurant is fully licensed.

The restaurant is also open to provide morning coffee and afternoon teas.

There is also a smaller dining room seating 60 which can be reserved for private parties.

The menu has no bias. From Chef Andy Devine, who has come from Weston-super-Mare, patrons will be able to get Indian, American, Continental and British dishes as well as specialities on various nights.

The whole menu will be a la carte and nothing will be pre-cooked. Two magnificent grills in the kitchen will stand by under the eye of the grill chef. (Cont Page 2...)

CELEBRATION DINNER MARKS THE OPENING

Oppulence and elegance are the standards set by the new Omega Restaurant – A sign of things to come.

BEHIND THE SCENES

Manager Micky Kikillarou is sure that he will be able to suit any taste – and he knows quite a bit about Sheffield palates and preferences after 26 years in the city.

The wine list will be as extensive as the menu. There will be 98 wines available besides other drinks diners may require. While waiting to take their tables for dinner they will get their aperitifs and cocktails in a comfortable bar connecting the foyer and restaurant.

The customers will also be able to see the care and preparation which goes on behind the scenes, for they will be allowed to visit the kitchen if they wish.

Everything from that lump of ice in your drink to the scampi on the table is prepared to match the surrounding luxury.

And that lump of ice is special. It is produced by an ice-making machine, manufactured in Britain on an American idea.

REQUESTS FOR BOOKINGS

The kitchen is tiled and designed for optimum hygiene. It has every desirable kitchen device and gives the chef plenty of space in which to work.

It is stocked up with top-class cutlery and china which will feature on the tables with silverware to complete the picture.

Mr. Milne feels that the Omega will fill a great gap in Sheffield's nightlife and facilities. Already he has been besieged by requests for bookings.

In every aspect of the Omega project he has tried to aim for perfection and he knows the high standard he has set.

The luxury is not superficial. It would have been easy enough to put in a few fake panelled walls but the wood of the Omega is real.

It would have been just as easy to have an elaborate restaurant with no additional comforts but even the deep-piled carpeted ladies' powder room has that same finish.

At a time when people all over the country are losing their reserve and savouring fully the pleasures of dining out, the Omega seems to have an especially important place.

Mr. Milne is quite candid about its purposes and the kind of people it will attract. It is expensive by present provincial standards. An evening out with your wife, a business friend or a girlfriend will not leave much change out of a "fiver".

But for the service they will get at the Omega Mr. Milne is sure they will have had value for money.

Roast duck and apricot sauce or Indian curries "the like of which Sheffield has never seen before."

These will be just two of the many appetising dishes guests at a private dinner tonight celebrating the opening of the Omega will be able to choose from.

But if you are not lucky enough to have an invitation, you will have the chance of sampling the food yourself when the restaurant opens to the public tomorrow.

Among the guests at the dinner will be the Lord Mayor and Lady Mayoress, Ald. And Mrs. P.J. Kirkman , the Deputy Lord Mayor, Ald. J.W. Sterland and Mrs. Sterland, the Director and General Manager of the Sheffield Telegraph and Star Ltd., Mr J.F. Goulden and Mrs. Goulden, the Assistant General Manager, Mr. J.G.S. Linacre and Mrs Linacre, and a director of the Sheffield Telegraph and Star Ltd., Mr. W. Lyth and Mrs. Lyth.

KITCHENS

Also there will be the Managing Director of Sheffield Refreshment Houses Ltd. (the Owners of the Omega), Mr S.R. Milne, and Mrs. Milne, with the chairman, Mr. H. Dixon and Mrs. Dixon, and the secretary and director, Mr. L. Lewis and Mrs. Lewis.

All the guests will be afforded the same privilege everyone will have at the Omega. If a special dish is required cooked a certain way, you can go into the kitchens and supervise the operation yourself.

A novel feature of the evening will be the presentation to every lady of a small gold bracelet charm in the form of the Greek letter Omega.

With the resident four-piece band will be the Foxhill Singers, a well-known local group.

SALMON

There will also be a luncheon this morning for businessmen and tradesmen of the city. And for the 100 guests there will be a buffet described in the words of Mr. Milne as "nicer than anything Sheffield has seen before."

Place of honour will go to a huge Boar's head and a giant salmon which appears to be swimming in water.

With the dinner at the Omega tonight there will be born a new experience for gourmets in the Sheffield area.

And for the added satisfaction of all the local people who might dine in the palatial surroundings of the restaurant, the silver cutlery with which they eat their meal was manufactured in Sheffield.

The bosses of Sheffield Refreshment Houses Ltd were the great and good of Sheffield, and included Sir Stuart Goodwin, one of the city's major benefactors. Among other things, he was chairman of the Fredrick's Hotel group which owned the Grand Hotel in Sheffield and the Cumberland in London. Sheffield Refreshment Houses also owned Kenwood Hall, St. Andrews Hotel and the Hunter House Hotel, all key establishments at the time.

In those days Sheffield's licensing was under the control of a watch committee and many of its members were connected to the Refreshment Houses group. So you can imagine the raised eyebrows when the Omega was granted a noon – 2am licence to operate Monday to Saturday. Locals were very concerned the company may have plans to open a night club at the venue. This was strongly denied in the press and gave the company another opportunity to get the Omega's name in the paper.

The influence exerted by Sheffield Refreshment Houses went further than just licensing. Because of their connections they were able to employ the best staff available in the city and quite a few out-of-towners too. They attracted several staff from the Grand Hotel and the Royal Victoria, the two most notable hotels at the time. It was imperative that they won over the clientele that frequented these establishments too. Trevor Wright recalls the moment when they knew those crucial customers were finally convinced;

'After the horrendous start there was a period of calm and it was as if people were saying "lets keep away, let them get their act together".

Lessons were learned and slowly but surely we started to perform like the first class restaurant we aspired to be. This was noticeable when some of Sheffield's captains of industry and other local celebrities started to book for lunch or dinner.

The waiting staff were a buzz with excitement one night. It appeared that Bob Stanley, a well known local businessman, had made a reservation. He was a Grand Hotel stalwart and here was our chance to make him an Omega regular.

He was given table five, a favourite table since it occupied a corner that gave it a certain cosiness and at the same time it offered an excellent view of the dance floor. Mr Stanley never took an aperitif in the lounge – he always went straight to his table.

On this, his first night at the Omega, the Maitre d', the station head waiter and the commis waiter all put their best foot forward to make this a night to remember for Mr Stanley and his guest. When it came to the dessert course, the Maitre d' announced that we had made his favourite, apple pie and custard, the way he always enjoyed it at The Grand.

He was, of course, delighted and sat there with a kindly smile and a great appreciation of the trouble the staff had gone to. The commis waiter was sent to the kitchen to bring out the famous apple pie. There was great ceremony while the Maitre d' portioned the pie and dribbled it with custard before serving it to Mr Stanley and his guest. This should have brought a glorious evening to a perfect end. Except the young waiter by mistake had picked up a turkey pie made for the staff supper. But all's well that end's well and Mr Stanley was very forgiving – so much that on his next visit he brought his own monogrammed cutlery which meant he was here to stay.

J. Trevor Wright

The Start of My Love Affair with the Omega

I am not sure if it was all the newspaper hype that got my attention or the idea of the new modern food style or just my yearning to be part of the most fashionable scene in Sheffield. But something about the place had struck a chord inside me that was never to leave. My love affair with the Omega started in 1963. I got a job there as a grill chef under John Mason, who to this day was one of the best chefs I have ever worked with. He was a perfectionist who would stand at the 'Pass' to inspect every single plate that left the kitchen. Along with his wife Olive, the pastry cook, they totally controlled everything. The Omega revelled in fantastic food, quality service and traditional cooking. John Mason was from the classic Escoffier school, taking his time over stocks and sauces. He insisted too that we hung our own beef to ensure it had the correct time to mature. John was also unusual for a chef in that he never lost his temper in the kitchen. There were no histrionics, something I can't claim myself.

The Omega was very good at providing the right food, service and atmosphere to make its customers feel special. From the moment diners arrived they were the focus of attention, initially greeted by the concierge and their cars parked by a team of valets, the perfect start to a fine evening. Among the regulars I remember was Mr Dawson, a materials man with a shop on Pinstone Street, Stanley Speight, the director of Sheffield Refreshment Houses. Among the other late and greats were Albert and Joan Bramall, Ted Horsewood and John Clixby, the owner of Baslow Hall, now Fischer's. At the time Sheffield had more Rolls-Royces and Bentleys than any other city and it wasn't long before they were parking outside the Omega on a regular basis. It quickly became the place to be seen.

In the 1960s dining out was largely the preserve of the business community, whose members used to love entertaining over lunch. There were also the 'nouveau riche' of the time who were discovering the pleasures of good food. The Omega under Sheffield Refreshment Houses did an incredible amount of business from the start but like all restaurants of its type, it suffered a hammer blow at the hands of the government. In my opinion the reason for the decline of lunching out was the Jim Callaghan budget of 1965 which penalised business entertaining expenses.

Before that budget business lunches were tax deductable. You could say they were free lunches paid for by the government, but the budget stopped all that. Trade was also affected by other newcomer upmarket establishments such as the Hallam Tower Hotel. The company closed the restaurant and sold the property to Sheffield businessman Stephen Hinchliffe in 1978. I had left well before trade began to drift away. I had only worked there for about 18 months. I thought I'd left virtually unnoticed until recently, when I received this letter from Trevor Wright, who recalls what he thought would be my last evening's work in the building.

"The intercom rings in the bar around midnight – it's Saturday and we've been busy and now the diners are on the dance floor – I answer the phone, it's Chef Mason who says "Trevor, it's David Baldwin's last night, can I bring him into the lounge for a drink?"

"Sure, I'll bet you miss him." I say.

"Well, yes and no," he said. "How come?" I ask. "Well he drives me crazy!" – "In what way?" I ask. "Well when the Maitre d' sends in a food order he sometimes writes their name on it and David will shout; "I know them." He makes it sound like he knows everyone in Sheffield!"

"Not to worry" I said, "Just bring him in." To which he replies, "Oh by the way, I must tell you that he's wearing that old cardigan and carpet slippers." I smiled and said, "that's David alright – but just go on and bring him in."

David was by the lounge exit doors and we all watched in utter amazement when almost everyone not only recognised him, but stopped to chat for a few minutes!

I'm not sure if you remember that night David, but I remember it well. In fact, Chef said later, "I take it back, he must know everybody in Sheffield!"

J. Trevor Wright

The Wheatsheaf, Parkhead

From those days as a grill chef I had pledged to myself that someday I would own the Omega. Perhaps it was the arrogance of youth, but somehow despite its early successes I thought I could do a better job of it than they could and I knew that the only way to make real money in our business was to become the gaffer. Sheffield Refreshment Houses had run the Omega as a high class restaurant and did the occasional wedding. I thought then it had a better and different future ahead of it – as a banqueting venue.

I was to run the popular pub the Wheatsheaf at Parkhead, then the Anglers Rest in Bamford with Pauline and finally the Hillsborough Suite at Sheffield Wednesday's Football Ground before I would realise this dream some 17 years after that final night as The Omega Restaurant grill chef.

The way we were... Recipes from 1964 Revived

I was recently given a copy of the 1964 Omega Valentine's night menu by Audrey Hobson, who remembers the evening with great fondness as it was on that day her engagement to her late husband Mike was announced. Looking at the menu, it was strange to think I was most probably in the kitchen on that very evening.

The price differences aside, this little piece of history shows that restaurant food hasn't changed as much as you might think. Of course, dishes may have a modern twist and are presented completely differently – we've inhabited a paper doily-free zone for years now – but nearly a lifetime later we still regularly serve many of the dishes that were a hit back in 1964. Following, are four fabulous courses updated for our current luncheon and banqueting menus that are timeless in their ability to please.

OMEGA RESTAURANT

HORS-D'OEUVRES

Caviare de Sevruga	23/-
Raviera des Hors D'oeuvre	5/6
Crevettes Marie Rose	5/-
Jambon de Parme and Melon	10/6
Pate Maison	5/-
Foie Gras de Strasbourg	28/-
Saumon Fume d'Ecosse	10/6
Smoked Trout	7/-
Potted Shrimps	5/-
Whitebait	6/6

POTAGES

Tortue Verte au Xeres	4/6
Lobster Bisquit	4/6
Creme Pompadour	3/-
Veloute Dame Blanche	3/-
Minestrone Milanaise	3/-

OEUFS eT PATES

Oeufs Poches Florentine	6/6
Oeufs A La Creme	6/-
Omelettes Selon Choix	9/6
Spaghetti Bolanaise	7/6
Spaghetti Napolitaine	6/6

POISSOINS

Goujonade de Sole Diable	10/6
Delice de Sole Waleska	14/6
Sole Doubres Maitre D'Hotel	13/6
Homard Neuburg	M.P.
Homard Thermidor	M.P.
Scampis Frites	14/-
Scampis Meuniere	14/-

GRILLADES

Fliete Steak Princess	15/6
Rump Steak	12/6
Entrecote Steak	14/-
Pot Pourri Omega	14/6
Cotellets d'Agneau	10/-
Grilled Gammon	12/6

SPECIALITES

Tornedo Monted'or	17/6
Tornedo Rossini	17/6
Escalopes Cordonbleu	14/6
Escalopes Ambassadeur	13/6
Supreme de Volaille Maryland	17/6
Supreme de Volaille A La Kiev	17/6
Duckling a l'Orange	16/6

SPECIALITIES
Cooked At Your Table.

Steak Omega	21/-
Steak A La Creme	20/-
Steak Diane	20/-
Chicken A La Creme	16/6
Escalope Veal Marsalla	17/6

LEGUMES

Pommes Croquettes	2/-
Pommes Lyonaise	2/-
Pommes Sautee	2/-
Broccoli Spears	3/-
Haricots Verts	2/6
Chou-Fleur au Gratin	3/-
Asparagus Tips	4/-

FLAMBEES

Crepes Susette
Ananas
Peches
Bananas

ENTREMENTES

Poire Dame Blanche	4/-
Peches Cardinal	4/-
Coupe Rothschild	4/6
Meringue Clace	4/-
Crepe Citron	4/-

CANAPES.

Canape Diane	4/6
Canape Woodcock	3/6
Welsh Rarebit	3/-
Canape au Champignons	3/-

Audrey Hobson,

Dear David,
I wondered if you would like this menu for your archives! Mike & I spent our engagement evening (big occasion) at the Omega and got the menu signed by the Head waiter. Look at the prices! It was Valentines day 1964 so its kept well.

Audrey

Dinner 22/6

Fresh Grapefruit *Cocktail*
Assorted Fruit Juices
Iced Melon
Consomme Profitrole
Creme Reine

.

Fillet of Sole Bonne Femme

.

Roast Norfolk Turkey, Stuffing, Chipolata and Cranberry Sauce
Roast Duckling, Orange Salad
Escalope of Veal Ambassadeur
Grilled Lamb Cutlet Princess
or Cold Buffet
Salmon
Beef
Ham
Tongue
Turkey
Duck
Chicken
Assorted Salad and Pickles

Peas a la Francaise
Haricots Verts
Lyonaise and Creamed Potatoes

.

Charlotte Russe
Sherry Trifle
Pear Gateau
Coupe Mikado
Various Ices
Scotch Woodcock

Cream 1s. 6d. extra
Cona Coffee 2s. 0d. extra
MINIMUM CHARGE 22/6

Ω

The ALPHA ROOM
is available for Wedding Receptions, Private Luncheons
and Dinners

Eggs Florentine à la Brincliffe

Oeufs Pochés Florentine – Serves 10 but cook 12 eggs in case you break one

An Italian classic dish and one of chef Mason's signature dishes from the Omega during the sixties. However the best I ever had was at a little place near Florence where Pauline and I had the good fortune to join the family for lunch at their Medici Villa alongside their vineyards and olive groves.

Ingredients

12 large free-range eggs

1 teaspoon of vinegar

2 teaspoons salt

Salt and pepper

800g fresh baby leaf spinach

200g Cheddar cheese

1 large bowl of iced water

For the Florentine sauce:

110g salted butter

170g plain flour

1 litre semi-skimmed milk

For serving:

10 ramekin dishes

Method

1. Half fill a large pan with water and bring to the boil. Add 2 teaspoons of salt and 1 teaspoon of vinegar. Turn down the heat to simmer.

2. Crack 2 eggs at a time into the water for 25 seconds just to seal the outside. Remove the eggs with a slotted spoon into ice cold water. You can leave them in the cold water until you've sealed all 12.

3. Remove the eggs carefully from the ice cold water onto a kitchen towel and drain off the excess water. Be careful not to break them.

4. Wash the spinach and dry well. Heat a pan and add a little oil, then drop the spinach into the pan and stir quickly with a spoon until it is just starting to wilt, then take out onto a plate.

5. To make the sauce, melt butter in a pan slowly, and then add flour to make a roux. Slowly add the milk until it reaches a coating consistency (it should coat the back of a wooden spoon).

6. Arrange spinach in bottom of ramekins, lay one egg on top and cover with Florentine Sauce, finish with cheese and bake for 12 minutes in a preheated oven at 180°c and serve.

7. Lovely served with a toasted English muffin!

Lobster Thermidor Baldwin's Style

Homard Thermidor – Serves 10, half a lobster per portion

One of my favourite dishes. So much so that I served it as the entrée at my 70th Birthday lunch for 70 of my oldest friends… also known as the Cocoa and Horlicks brigade.

Ingredients

5 x 500g live lobsters

1 pint of Thermidor sauce (see below)

Chopped fresh parsley

3 large potatoes, mashed with butter

1 cup of grated, good quality, fresh Parmesan cheese

For the Thermidor sauce:

110g salted butter

110g plain flour

1 litre semi-skimmed milk

110g Cheddar cheese

Teaspoon of Coleman's English mustard

Method

1. Half fill a large pan with water and bring to the boil. When boiling, pierce the back of the head of each lobster with a knife then submerge into boiling water. Bring back to the boil then reduce the heat to simmering. Simmer for 20 minutes, drain off into a colander and allow to cool by plunging into ice-cold water. (If you don't want to cook the lobsters you can buy them already cooked from the fishmonger but they will not be as tender).

2. Peel and boil the potatoes until soft, drain and mash the potato and add butter to mash until smooth.

3. To make the sauce, melt butter in a pan slowly, and then add flour and mustard to make a roux. Slowly add the milk until it reaches a coating consistency. Stir in the cheese.

4. Split the lobsters in half lengthways, being careful to keep the shell intact. Remove all the meat, cut into one inch pieces and put to one side. Discard the parts from inside the head. Also crack the claws and remove all the meat from them. Slice the meat as above.

5. Place the shells onto a baking sheet and pipe mashed potato the full length of the shell. Arrange the pieces of lobster inside the shell on top of the mashed potato, and smother with the Thermidor sauce, parsley and Parmesan.

6. Bake in a pre-heated hot oven approximately 170°c for 12-15 minutes until bubbling hot. Flash under a red hot grill to colour and serve.

Chef Roebuck's Famous Tournedos Rossini

Stephen's Rossini varies slightly from the classical as we prefer to use more ethically produced chicken livers rather than foie gras. But rest assured even when served for 300 the taste is 'estupendo'.

Ingredients

10 x 110g fillet steaks, tenderised and rolled up. Trim the meat and keep the trimmings

4 slices white sliced bread, for croutons

500g chicken liver paté (see below for recipe)

1 medium white onion

20 shallots, for roasting

450g beef bones

1 carrot

2 sticks celery

Half a leek

4 peppercorns

2 tablespoons olive oil

For the sauce:

100ml Madeira

100ml red wine

4 sprigs of thyme

1 clove of garlic

For the paté:

1kg chicken livers, trimmed and de-veined

2 medium onions, finely chopped

5 cloves of garlic, chopped

200g butter

1 glass of cooking brandy

Splash of double cream

Sprinkle of mixed herbs

Method

1. Roast some beef bones in the oven at 180°c for 30 minutes until golden brown.
2. Transfer the bones to a pan with chopped onion, carrot, celery, leek, peppercorns, and cover with 2 pints of water. Keep the tray for roasting the shallots.
3. Boil rapidly for 20 minutes then turn down the heat and simmer until the liquid has reduced by half. Pass through a strainer and put the stock to one side.
4. Peel shallots and place in the tray from the bones. Place shallots in a hot oven with olive oil, salt, thyme sprigs and roast for 30 minutes until golden brown and tender.
5. Meanwhile, to make the sauce, fry trimmings from the fillet steaks in a pan with onion, thyme and garlic, until light brown. Add a tablespoon of plain flour to make a roux. Add the beef stock and the red wine and reduce by half. Check the seasoning and pass through a strainer once more. Leave to simmer away until you are ready to fry the steaks.
6. Cut 10 neat square croutons out of the white sliced bread and pan fry in a little olive oil until golden brown.
7. Slice 10 pieces of chicken liver paté and place back into the fridge.
8. Meanwhile in a frying pan add a little oil. When hot, sear your first steaks on all sides until golden brown and remove into an oiled baking tray. Repeat this until all steaks are sealed. Season with salt and black pepper.
9. When your shallots are halfway through cooking, add steaks to the oven for 12 minutes. This will cook the meat medium/rare. When the steaks have been cooking for 10 minutes, place a slice of chicken liver pate on to each steak roll. Cook for the remaining 2 minutes.
10. To finish your sauce, add Madeira. Flambé if you wish and season to taste.
11. Lay out warm plates. Place croutons on the bottom, the steak and paté on top, drizzle over the sauce and add the roasted shallots.

For the chicken liver paté:

1. Cook the livers, onions and butter in a heavy bottomed sauce pan. Reduce heat and simmer for around one hour.
2. Add the brandy and cook for a further 10 minutes to evaporate the alcohol. Turn off the heat and remove the lid.
3. When cooled to room temperature, place all ingredients from the pan into a food processor and blitz until smooth, adding a good splash of double cream to lighten.
4. Divide the mix into ten pot ramekins and smooth the top with a palette knife. Top with melted butter and place in the fridge to set.
5. Serve with crisp salad, fruit chutney and loads of toast or use for the Tournedos Rossini.

Crêpes Suzette à la Big 'Un

Possibly one of my greatest achievements in large-scale cooking is getting 300 crêpes to the table looking and tasting like they have all just jumped out of the pan. They are great flamed in brandy and served with double cream and vanilla ice cream.

Ingredients

For the crêpes:

140g sugar

140g plain flour

140g melted unsalted butter

5 medium free-range eggs

1 tablespoon of tepid milk

For the sauce:

50g butter

100g brown sugar

30g flour

850ml orange juice

3 standard measures of Grand Marnier

Segments of 3 oranges

Method

1. Crack the eggs into a bowl and whisk until the yolks are broken, then gradually add the rest of the crêpe ingredients and mix into a smooth batter.

2. Using a flat heavy-bottomed frying pan, melt a knob of butter and add enough batter to cover the bottom of the pan. Fry lightly on each side until golden brown. Remove the crêpe from the pan and set to one side. Repeat this process until all the mixture has gone and you have enough pancakes. Place greaseproof paper between each pancake to ensure they don't stick together.

3. To make the sauce, combine the butter and the sugar in a heavy-bottomed pan. Cook until the sugar is dissolved. Add the flour to make a roux. Gradually add the orange juice and finish with Grand Marnier to a thickish consistency. Flambé the sauce if you wish. Add orange segments to the sauce.

4. Fold the crêpes into quarters and smother with the sauce. Serve with vanilla ice cream.

Baldwin's Omega
A Difficult Birth...

The original 'For Sale' photograph featured in The Sheffield Telegraph. Reproduced with kind permission from Sheffield Newspapers Ltd.

The Purchase

In 1981 Pauline and I were running the Hillsborough Suite at Sheffield Wednesday. And we were both frustrated. We had a successful formula which we longed to take to a bigger venue. We had tried to buy the Omega when it came up for sale in 1978 but we were outbid and it seemed our long-standing dream of owning the place was never to be realised. Following this disappointment we bought the Sheaf View at Heeley, where we intended to build a banqueting suite. The builders were already on site in 1981, when Pauline and I were dining In London at the Variety Club International convention. I was there in my capacity as Chairman of the South Yorkshire and Midlands tent. It was all routine stuff. I could have had no inkling that before we'd reached the dessert course, fate would conspire to change my life forever.

Out of the blue a telephone call came through from a Sheffield solicitor. The Omega restaurant and site buildings were once again on the market and would we be interested? Momentarily forgetting our project at the Sheaf View, we opened negotiations and within a few days we had agreed a price with the vendor, Stephen Hinchliffe. Pauline and I have always been impetuous when buying property. Our guiding principle has always been buy now, and think about the consequences later.

Suddenly, I was within touching distance of realising my greatest ambition. I'd harboured the idea of one day buying the Omega ever since I had worked there as a grill chef in those hurly-burly days of the early 1960s. It's a fortunate man who succeeds in attaining what he strives for. And I was lucky in another way too. As usual I was fully supported by Pauline. We were in full agreement that we should buy the place and put every effort and penny we had in to making the dream a reality.

The Dream

The Omega had failed as an upmarket restaurant. Our vision was to have a lunchtime venue but with banqueting as our main service, a scheme most of our friends thought was utter madness. We wanted to build on our banqueting experiences at the Anglers Rest and the Hillsborough Suite where we had developed our famous oven-to-table banqueting, serving truly fresh hot quality food with exemplary service to boot.

We sold the Hillsborough Suite to singer Tony Christie and his partner, and enjoyed an added boost when our loyal client base followed us to the Omega. Without the loyalty of these many supporters we would never have got the place off the ground.

We opened in 1981 and like all start-ups the first nine months were difficult and were not helped by a contractual disagreement with the vendor that left us with no rear access to the property. Consequently there was no access for emergency vehicles which meant that due to health and safety regulations we would have had our licence revoked at the April licensing sessions. We were left in a position where we needed to find funds. They were not available through normal channels. And so it was that my dear friends Ashley Turner and Don Lyon, who I knew from Sheffield's Junior Chamber of Commerce, stepped in and put together a rescue plan to buy the land we required to gain the vital access. In early March 1982 Hillsborough Suite Ltd was liquidated as a result of the contractual problems and Baldwin's Omega Ltd was born with new board members of Ashley, Don, myself and Pauline. We made a strong team and to this day Ashley and Don remain a great support.

During this difficult time we had also had terrific backing from our longstanding suppliers. We also had a small but very loyal management team led by Janet Wilson, who is still playing her part today and our mentor, the accountant Sandy Bethell. But without Ashley and Don there would be no Baldwin's Omega. Both are still directors of the company and we would like to thank them for their kindness, guidance and advice. There has always been a great relationship between us and we have never had a cross word.

During 1982 the phoenix rose. In sharp contrast to Christmas 1981, when the post was full of final demands mixed with a mere handful of greetings cards, 12 months later there was not a single demand, let alone a writ. But Christmas cards were there by the dozen and, best of all, lots of cheques. I sat in the office singing out loud 'what a difference a year makes!!'

We had emerged as Sheffield's leading banqueting house. From then on, we would always be moving forward, and that commitment to progress was reflected in an unbroken run of 25 years that saw figures improving year on year. When I'm asked what the secret behind that achievement is, I always say there is no secret. There's nothing mysterious about hard work.

Making a Name for Ourselves

There are few good times to start a new business, but 1981 was definitely not one of them, apart from the contractural difficulties there were other challenges. The country was not in a great financial shape, and nowhere was this more keenly felt than in Sheffield. The city's traditional steel industry was beset by closures and depression was everywhere.

But we had invested every penny we had into the Omega so there was no time for gloom. We had to make it a goer, and quickly. As soon as we turned the key in the door of the boarded-up restaurant we knew we'd done the right thing. The Omega was the kind of place, even full of dust and down at heel, that had a good atmosphere.

And we had a head start thanks to some business from our previous venue at Hillsborough, from where we moved all the pre-booked events to the Omega. One of our first marketing projects was to go back to all our contacts from the Wheatsheaf in the 1960s and the Anglers Rest days in the 1970s, where we had been famous for Sunday lunches. We launched our Sunday razzmatazz family days with past customers, friends and families.

Families would arrive at the Omega at 1pm and partake of a great Sunday lunch buffet, accompanied by live music and clowns to entertain the kids. We cast aside the old saying that there's no such thing as a free lunch. We didn't make a great deal of profit from them as we gave a lot of the lunches away. But it was all in the name of our marketing drive, and it worked. We used any excuse to celebrate; American Independence Day, Bastille Day, Yorkshire Day, you name it. The Omega was now drawing everyone from completely new customers through to those for whom our special events brought back memories of our Sundays at the Anglers Rest.

The Directors... friends indeed

FOR a change this week we decided to try a dinner dance—the package deal of the catering trade. We chose the Angler's Rest at Bamford, a favourite spot for Sheffielders and for tourists fresh from a day in the Derbyshire countryside, where they do a five-course meal with dancing, for £2.50 inclusive. While the Angler's also has a separate dining room for those who want an a la carte meal, our ratings refer to the dinner dance in the ballroom only—Graham Thorpe.

My menu

Prawn cocktail
Cream of vegetable soup
Roast turkey, Cranberry sauce, chipolata and vegetables
Ice cream
Coffee, mints
£2.50 per person standard charge inclusive of VAT and service
Bottle of Chablis (£1.80)

The meal

Perhaps we were unfortunate in sitting where we did, but every time the pianist launched into his selection from the Sound of Music the table jumped up and down.

But it would by churlish to complain, live music-while-you-eat is comparitively rare these days.

Tables are set round the dance floor in the ballroom and on a raised section at one end of the room.

There's a standard charge of £2.50 a person for the Saturday night dinner dances — and that helps a lot when it comes to choosing from the five-course menu, none of that

business of choosing by price instead of by dish.

From a generous selection of starters we both plumped for prawn cocktail. Soup's the same for everyone (and home-made) so that was easy.

From the half-dozen main course dishes I went for turkey and my wife — still a meat-eater despite the prices our local butcher charges — ordered the fillet of beef.

There was a standard brew of vegetables: Three sorts of potatoes, peas, carrots and cauliflower in cheese sauce.

The turkey came ready equipped with stuffing, Cranberry sauce and a chipolata. The beef was topped with mushrooms in sauce.

That little lot answered to most Yorkshiremen's description of a proper meal — good whole ome food and plenty of it. A bottle of Chablis (£1.80) helped it all on its way.

Nothing really fancy to choose for the sweet, but after the amount we had eaten it would have been wasted on us anyway. So we had ice cream which came with chocolate sauce to make it more interesting.

Coffee rounded things off — served, like the soup had been, from a table to one side of the ballroom. There was fresh cream with it but no choice of Gaelic or any of those exotic coffees (for £2.50 all in how could

The Angler's Rest

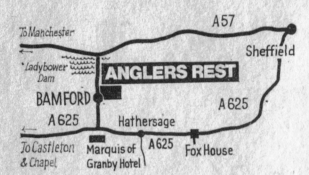

How to get there

From Sheffield you can take either the A625 Chapel road (via Fox House and Hathersage) or A57 Manchester road (turning off at Ladybower) depending which part of the city you are setting out from. From the city centre it is about the same by either route.

there be) so we ordered brandy (25p) and pretended.

By this time the pianist had called it a day, the main lights were turned off and candles were brought to the tables.

Until a couple of months ago, dancing was to a trio. Now its to pop records played by Popcorn, a mobile discotheque. The clientele appreciate the change in tempo according to "mine host" David Baldwasn't until next day that win.

Certainly on the night we were there the predominantly young crowd were all up and dancing.

One point to remember when you're budgeting for the evening, dancing is thirsty work.

Service throughout was first class, sometimes almost too quick for the digestion, and the only real grumble was that the ballroom looked as if it had seen better days and some of the furniture and fittings were obviously due for retirement.

The management recognise this and help is on the way. The ballroom is to be redecorated soon, in similar style to the new a la carte dining room upstairs — with sandblasted Derbyshire stone walls and cottage furniture giving a more sophisticated touch.

I wouldn't call it a complaint, but they forgot to charge us for the wine. It I realised — and a cheque is now on the way

Entertainment

There is a dinner dance every Saturday night and the ballroom (which holds 80) is used several nights a week for private functions. The bar locals make their own entertainment — they have two darts and two dominoes teams.

About the

Anglers Rest

The Anglers manages to retain a split personality, combining the atmosphere of a country pub with facilities of pub bar, ballroom and modern restaurant.

It has been run for the last three years by Mr. David Baldwin, who used to manage the Wheatsheaf at Ecclesall.

You can buy hot or cold snacks in the bar, dinner dances and Sunday lunches are held in the ballroom and swish a la carte meals are served in the Ashopton Room.

This was opened last year, has its own bar and seats about 40. A feature of the restaurant is a big open log fire.

The menu carries a blurb about the nearby village of Ashopton which was flooded to make Ladybower — and from that you would guess rightly that the Anglers gets a good number of American tourists.

Apparently they like to take the menu, with its little bit of potted history, back home to Ma.

The Anglers used to be residential but the bedrooms were knocked out to make way for the restaurant.

The large car park at the back can cope with all but the bueiest of evenings.

Points of interest

The Anglers is one of the oldest eating houses in Derbyshire. It was built as a hostelry and watering place in 1725 when Bamford was on the salt route from Cheshire.

Parts of the original building have been preserved and are incorporated in the present one. Before the dams were built the river used to run nearby — hence the name.

Ratings guide

★★★★★ SUPERB

★★★★ VERY GOOD

★★★ GOOD

★★ AVERAGE

★ POOR

The First Innings

Our first job from the Omega kitchen was an outside catering contract. We did a lot of outside catering in those days, a business that didn't last for several reasons. For a start we never learned how to charge properly and the hassle was never worth the income. The day we first used our kitchen was for an outside catering event in a marquee in Abbeydale Park. It was the Sheffield Collegiate Cricket Club Centenary Dinner for 300 people. We were having the second course of soup delivered from the Omega kitchen and telephoned the restaurant to signal it was time for it to set off as we served the starter. The plan was to give adequate time for the soup to make the journey to Abbeydale Park and still be hot enough to serve. During the first and second courses the crowd were to be entertained by the Bolsterstone Male Voice Choir. They had just one or two songs prepared but when our soup got stuck in traffic due to a car accident the crowd were treated to 45 minutes of the choir, a long but entertaining break between courses. I just kept shouting 'more, more' and had all the staff clap loudly as if that was what the clients wanted. We also lost 300 spoons that day so the profit was swallowed up straight away.

The following year of 1982 brought more challenges as yet more of the city's big companies went to the wall. So we had to find new customers. Once again we turned to an idea that had worked well at Hillsborough. If the corporate business was getting hard to come by, then we had to offer something to attract the people of Sheffield.

CENTENARY 1981

SHEFFIELD COLLEGIATE C.C.
1881

CELEBRATION DINNER AT
ABBEYDALE PARK, SHEFFIELD
THURSDAY, 18TH JUNE 1981

CRICKET WEEK SPONSORED BY
BARCLAYS BANK

Menu

Roulardes of Smoked Salmon "Fleetwood"
(Smoked Scotch Salmon garnished with large Mediterranean prawns)
La Ina Sherry

—

Spring Vegetable Soup

—

Yorkshire Hors d'Oeuvre "Baldwin"
(Yorkshire Pudding with rich gravy and Onion Sauce)
Calvert Blanc

—

Medallions of Beef "Geoffrey Boycott"
New Potatoes
Whole Green Beans
Pepper Salad
Calvert Rouge

—

Fresh Strawberries "Abbeydale"
with Dairy Cream

—

Stilton
"Old" Tawny Port

—

Coffee

Toasts

THE QUEEN

—

"CRICKET & SHEFFIELD COLLEGIATE"
PROPOSED BY CANON SMITH, VICAR OF BURY.
RESPONSE BY C. G. BUCK ESQ.
PRESIDENT SHEFFIELD COLLEGIATE.

—

"THE NEXT HUNDRED YEARS"
PROPOSED BY CHRIS MARTIN JENKINS,
B.B.C. CRICKET COMMENTATOR.
RESPONSE BY MIKE STEVENSON,
CRICKET REPORTER "DAILY TELEGRAPH."

CHAIRMAN D. G. FLEETWOOD.

CHORAL AND MUSICAL INTERLUDES BY
THE BOLSTERSTONE MALE VOICE CHOIR AND
THE THURLSTONE BRASS BAND.

SHEFFIELD COLLEGIATE
CRICKET CLUB CENTENARY
1981
PROGRAMME OF EVENTS

Saturday, 20th June
Collegiate Third XI v Old Edwardians
2.00 pm start at Abbeydale.

Sunday, 21st June
Collegiate Second XI v Harrogate
2.00 pm start at Abbeydale.

Monday, 22nd June
Chairman's XI v Colts
4.30 pm start at Abbeydale.

Tuesday, 23rd June
Collegiate v MCC
11.30 am – 6.30 pm.

Wednesday, 24th June; Thursday, 25th June
Collegiate v Devon Touring Side
11.30 am – 6.30 pm.

Friday, 26th June
Collegiate v Yorkshire League Side
2.00 pm start.

Saturday, 27th June
Collegiate First XI v Scarborough
Yorkshire League 2.00 pm start at Abbeydale.

Sunday, 28th June
Collegiate Fourth XI v Ashover
2.30 pm start at Abbeydale.

Sheffield Collegiate CC Centenary dinner, the menu from our first catering job at Baldwin's way back in June 1981.

Party Nights

Party Nights

We started party nights at the Omega. I then borrowed an idea from Muriel, the famous caterer at Abbeydale Sports Club. Salmon and strawberry parties were an instant hit, and we still do around 2000 covers at these evenings during the quieter summer months. Our other summer success came about as I was sunning myself by the pool at the Aigua Blava Hotel on the Costa Brava. I wondered what would happen to our summer trade if salmon and strawberry crops ever failed and thankfully I had this wonderful vision whilst looking up at the palm trees that surrounded the hotel pool. Let's do authentic Caribbean food, served up to the sound of a steel band. I often say that this stroke of holiday inspiration meant that holiday should have been tax deductable. Shame the Inland Revenue don't see it that way. I am just happy we are still doing 1500 Caribbean night covers a year with a crew who are now mainly the sons of our original Caribbean show band. Recently things have hotted up with the addition of a fire-defying limbo dancer.

Many theme nights were to follow many of these originating from our own family holiday influences, Spanish nights, Italian nights, disco nights and dinner dances. One of our most successful themed dinner dances was born in the early nineties. Before this time January was a good month for us as many companies used to have their annual staff party then, the recession of 1991 put paid to that.

We desperately needed something to celebrate so we had to put our thinking caps on. Out of the blue, our good friends David Biggs and Peter Stewart asked us to do a gentlemen's Burns night dinner for 20 guests in our smaller private room, and the germ of an idea emerged. Why not while holding the private Burns night dinner in our smaller room, hold a public Burns night alongside it in the ballroom. But how to get it off the ground? Simple – we sent a letter to everybody in the Sheffield phone book whose surname began with 'Mac' or 'Mc'. The reaction was in the true spirit of that legendary Scottish readiness to spend freely. We sold out three nights straight away. It was one of the saviours in that recession and we've continued to build it up over the years, sometimes having eight or nine Burns night dinner dances which account for more haggis than Gleneagles Hotel gets through, to the astonishment of our friends north of the border. The menu is the same each year. It includes real MacSween's of Edinburgh haggis, which is of course piped in, we always have a Ceildh band and they are often the best nights of the year. We raise a glass to the great man – and to his mother for giving birth to him in January.

Our most recent addition to our themed calendar is the barbeque evening sponsored by Pimms, who kindly supplied the barbeque that makes them possible. Party nights all continue to do well because of our focus on really great authentic food and value for money for an inclusive and entertaining night out. My personal favourites are always the wine evenings. But more about those later...

*Classic Dinner Party Menus
of the Eighties*

Ladybower Smoked Trout Fillets with Horseradish Cream

Serves 10 people

In the seventies and eighties we served this popular dish on a plate in strips but in these modern times best use a tall glass to impress your dinner party guests. This dish is easy to prepare early and leave in the fridge until you are ready to serve.

Ingredients

10 fresh smoked trout fillets

100ml double cream

110g mayonnaise

1 dessert spoon horseradish

1 teaspoon chopped dill

2 and a half lemons

Salad leaves

Half a cucumber

20 cherry tomatoes

10 radishes

Method

1. To make sauce; in a bowl, blend mayonnaise, the juice of half a lemon, horseradish, double cream and dill. Whisk until fully combined. Place in the fridge to rest.

2. Finely slice the radish and cucumber and combine with half of the cherry tomatoes. Split the 2 remaining lemons into 10 wedges, 1 per portion.

3. Arrange the leaves in a cocktail glass. Place alternate layers of cucumber, radish slices and trout in the glass and spoon on the horseradish sauce. Garnish with the remaining cherry tomatoes and a wedge of lemon.

4. Serve with fresh brown bread.

Escoffier's Historic Sole Véronique

Even I do not mess around with the great Escoffier's dishes. This is perfect for an entrée course.

Ingredients

6 x 170g fresh sole fillets,
skinned and trimmed, rolled skin
side in

For the fish sauce:

1 litre of fish stock

110g salted butter

170g plain flour

20ml double cream

1 onion, finely chopped

250g halved grapes

Salt and pepper to taste

Fresh dill for garnish

For the fish stock:

1 litre of water

Fish skins and trimmings

Half a glass white wine

Parsley stalks

Thick slice of lemon

Method

1. To make the stock, place all the ingredients in a pan and bring to the boil. Simmer for 20 minutes. Remove from the heat and drain the liquid through a sieve into a bowl. Discard the remainder.

2. To make the sauce, melt the butter in a heavy bottomed pan and add the onion, cook slowly until the onion is soft without any colour. Add the flour to make a roux. Slowly add the fish stock until it reaches a coating consistency, though make sure you retain some stock to poach the fish in, then add double cream and halved grapes. Season to taste.

3. Poach the sole in simmering fish stock for 5-6 minutes. Take out and drain well.

4. Place into a warm serving bowl, coat with sauce and serve with freshly chopped dill.

A French Peasants Classic
Farmhouse Chicken Chasseur

This dish was lovingly prepared for the men of the family particularly in winter when they returned from hunting and foraging for food to sustain the family. It is best served with a glass or two of Syrah wine from the north of the Côtes du Rhône region.

Ingredients

*10 x 170g chicken supreme, skin on, bone parred
(Use corn-fed chicken for that authentic French taste)*

1 large onion, roughly chopped

150g sliced mushrooms

100g plain flour

50g salted butter

6 tomatoes

Tablespoon of tomato purée

570ml chicken stock

Salt and pepper

Glass of red wine

Handful of chopped parsley

Method

1. Skin tomatoes by dropping in boiling water for 5 seconds and then refresh in cold water. Remove the skin and dice into small cubes.
2. In a pan add the butter and sweat the onions, mushrooms and a little salt and pepper until cooked without browning. Add the flour to make a roux, and then add the glass of red wine, tomato purée and slowly start adding chicken stock until you reach a thickish consistency. Add the chopped tomatoes and parsley.
3. Meanwhile, in a frying pan heat a little oil, then sauté the chicken breast skin side down for 2-3 minutes until starting to brown. Turn over and cook for the same amount of time on the other side, place into a hot preheated oven, around 180°c for 20 minutes.
4. Remove the chicken from the oven and rest for 5 minutes. Transfer to serving plates and smother with chasseur sauce.
5. Serve with fresh vegetables in season

Granny Baldwin's Trifle

Every time we serve this it brings back good memories of my childhood Sunday afternoon teatimes at home on Broomhall Street and Washington Road.

Ingredients

5 sponge fingers

3 punnets fresh raspberries

100ml sherry

For the jelly:

320ml water

2 sheets gelatine

3 tablespoons port

100g caster sugar

For the custard:

2 eggs

100g caster sugar

50g flour

10g custard powder

1 vanilla pod

For the topping:

500ml double cream (whipped)

Method

1. Divide the sponge fingers between 10 cocktail glasses and place in the bottom and soak in the sherry. Take half of the raspberries and scatter a few into each glass. Keep the rest aside.
2. For the jelly, cover the gelatine sheets with some water in a tin until soft. Meanwhile, boil the water, port and sugar in a pan.
3. When the gelatine is soft, drain, add it to the water and mix well. Pour over the sponge and leave in the fridge to set overnight.
4. For the custard, whisk the eggs and sugar in a bowl until almost white. Combine with the flour and custard powder. Heat the milk in a pan. When it has boiled, whisk on to the eggs, sugar and flour mixture and whisk together. Return to the cleaned pan and stir to the boil. Add the seeds from half a vanilla pod.
5. Put the mixture on top of the jelly and leave to set. Once cold, top with whipped cream and decorate with the remaining raspberries.

In Pursuit of Perfection

The Realisation of the Dream

Right from the start Pauline and I knew what we wanted from the newly-named Baldwin's Omega. The fine dining experience would remain for the lunchtime trade and the evenings would give way to banqueting. We would cater for weddings, birthdays and other celebrations. The aim was to make Baldwin's nothing short of the leading banqueting house in the north of England.

We had three weapons in our armoury to help achieve this. Outstanding service was first on the list. To go with it, we set our stall out for a modern British food style, where the use of fresh products sourced as locally as possible would be the utmost priority.

And so our motto was born, and it still holds good today; "Your special occasion deserves our attention."

Pauline and I are and have always been a team. The front of house food service and front office are her domain. My role is to get to grips with developing our bar and wine services and of course producing a kitchen brigade serving food to be proud of. Banqueting services are tricky to get right and our desire to serve fresh, hot, oven to table food for 300, that is as fresh and hot as a meal for four makes it even more of a challenge. Pauline developed our style of banqueting service that has since been imitated, rarely equalled and certainly never bettered. It is what we do best, and we've earned a nationwide reputation for it.

Chefs, including myself, have a saying when it comes to the tricky task of making the whole complex operation work. "It has to be the rider running the horse and not the horse running the rider" they will say, with the rider being the kitchen. Nice saying, but it doesn't work that way. If the kitchen is running the show the opinions and wishes of the customer are often ignored or just simply forgotten about. The kitchen after all cannot see how fast people are eating or know if they need a break between meals to play a game or make a speech unless front of house let them know. Pauline will tell you that the secret to running a smooth service is communication. The front of house and the kitchen must run as equals and learn to compromise. It is down to the front of house to work out when they think the customer wants each course and convey this to the kitchen. This requires shrewd judgement.

Baldwin's is always at its best when we have a tricky do. We have a meeting the day before with the head chef and the top tier of management to work the service out together. Like generals before a battle, we plan the operation and ensure the channels of communication are clear.

In all of this, the front line troops are primed for the task ahead. It has always been considered impolite to start serving different tables at different times during a banquet. The etiquette with traditional silver service is to serve each table equally with one waitress per table. First they serve warm plates then the meat then the vegetables and then the gravy, each time returning to the kitchen to collect the next item to be served.

The problem with this system is that by the time the server returns to the table with the next item the previous one has started to go cold. To solve this problem it is the fashion in London to serve banquet meals already plated. Everything is put on one plate in the kitchen and served at once. Quite often for a large banquet the food is plated early and reheated just before serving. Neither of these methods are used at Baldwin's. Reheating food was and will never be our style – fortunately Pauline developed her own system that ensures our customers get fresh hot food every time.

Pauline's Conveyor Belt System

Pauline's famous conveyor belt system was developed while we were at the Anglers Rest in Bamford during the 1970s. We had a banquet for approximately 70 people and several members of our staff had not turned in. With only four servers, comprising of Pauline, Janet Wilson and two thirteen year old twins, we were under pressure. Pauline decided to abandon old-fashioned etiquette in favour of serving our food hot and fresh to each table. Starting with the top table one of the twins put the warm plates down. She was immediately followed by Pauline serving the meat then Janet with the veg and the second twin served the gravy. We served the banquet one table at a time so that each table received everything hot and fresh from the kitchen. This is now common practice but back then it was so out of the norm that Pauline had to persuade the clients that it was ok to start eating their meal once everyone on their table had been served and that they didn't have to wait for the rest of the tables in the room. They tucked in and enjoyed the occasion.

Nowadays we still adhere to the same basic system although Pauline has developed it much further. We now serve as much as we can in the room with the chefs carving the meat in front of the clients. With any hot meals plated in the room, our clients can be sure the food is as fresh as it should be. Pauline and the team have the service down to a fine art which helps us stand out from the rest. We know exactly how many covers each service station can handle, how many staff we need per station to get the optimum level of service and how many stations the kitchen can handle to keep the food fresh. Of course, these vital figures must remain our trade secret.

Called to the Bar

I think I best sum up my principles with the way I've interviewed bar staff over many years. It is 50 years since I had my first Justices' licence with only one short break between 1962 to 1964, when I was still in the business but working for someone else.

My interview method is to sit at the end of a room and have applicants walk towards me. I watch the style and confidence of the walk and above all, take note of whether they smile. I always say "your smile is your fortune and mine". This is more than just a matter of good practice, how often have you walked into a pub or bar and been turned on or off in those first few seconds?

The guiding principles of running a good pub or restaurant bars is smiling staff, adherence to the strictest rules of cleanliness and selling the best products around. I have always insisted we serve the brand leaders – Coca-Cola in a glass bottle, Schweppes tonic served cold from a bottle in the fridge and Britvic fruit juices. Nothing less than proprietary brand spirits will do. I have no time for dubious labels. Keep it smart, keep it clean and stick to your brands.

The Rib Room at Lunch

Out to Lunch

There was one other vital ingredient in the Omega formula, and that came in the shape of the Rib Room, our luncheon restaurant. It's been there since the beginning, and for two good reasons. For one thing, it brings the building to life during the day when no major function is being held. And secondly, it gives the chefs a chance to showcase the food diners can expect at their event.

From the very beginning we put the emphasis on fresh food with daily roast joints and other dishes. We put our own slant on traditional British food – stews, terrines, Yorkshire hors d'oeuvres, the list goes on. For the first few years the restaurant was the preserve of groups like The Queens Street Club who would gather at the end of the week for the 'God bless Friday' lunch. The membership was made up of a select group of Sheffield legal high-flyers.

Groups like theirs thrived in the days when everyone had time for lunch. Originally we only had an à la carte menu but in the early nineties, after one of my little trips to France we started our 'plat du jour' menu which attracts a more social gathering for lunch. Our 'plat du jour' menu now complements our à la carte menu and the business style lunch finds favour with many ladies who lunch and others social diners.

Quality on our Doorstep

Each day since the luncheon restaurant opened we have always offered a selection of fresh fish, from our renowned cod and chips through to grilled halibut, Dover sole, lobster and crab. Everything is delivered fresh daily from William Howe and Co. of Maltravers Drive, Sheffield. Like our meat supplier, our fish merchant is second to none in Sheffield. They have fresh fish delivered daily from Grimsby docks and we always have a selection of what is best from the day's catch for the lunchtime specials board. We have had a great working relationship with the boys at William Howe's for many years and know we can rely on their judgement to send us the best of the day's catch. One of our chefs will still sometimes pop in to see them on the way to work to have a look over the fish. It's important to keep a personal eye on all your suppliers.

The menu also features at least one lamb dish, for which we can rely on fantastic supplies. The quality of lamb available today is light years better than ever before, largely due to the fact that farmers have developed two lambing seasons – the traditional one in spring and also one in autumn, thus allowing us to buy first class quality young lamb all year round.

We source only locally-produced chicken and game, including produce from local estates such as Chatsworth and Roche Abbey, not to mention fine venison from Round Green Farm near Barnsley. All in all, we have access to an abundance of great produce from nature's table.

The improved standards of husbandry in the pig industry and the availability of rare breeds has led to the production of exceptional quality pork for the table. In the 1980s we sold a lot of suckling pig, which is not as popular now but we still serve it from time to time. Some may prefer to cook fancy dishes with pork, but I firmly believe it should be cracklingly fresh with bramley apple sauce, sage and onion stuffing and a good sausage with rich pork gravy.

Thanks to the new passport cattle system and the much-improved care for animals from our beef farmers we now have plentiful supply as well as our ever-popular calf's liver with fried onions and bacon, a permanent fixture on our à la carte menu, cooked how the customer likes it.

Over the years we have developed our pâtisserie skills and desserts are now all made on the premises and of course our home-made bread that is freshly baked that morning ready to be served complimentary with your lunch. What you don't eat with your lunch you can take home for your tea.

We are most famous for our roast sirloin of beef and it is always on the menu carved at your table with real Yorkshire pudding.

Oxford and Blacks, pedigree pigs from the Peak District

Lunchtime Favourites

Yorkshire Hors D'Oeuvres

Serves 10, using 3 inch Yorkshire pudding tins, 1 medium pudding per portion

This cornerstone of British cooking is known at Baldwin's as Yorkshire hors d'oeuvres, and it regularly appears on our lunch menu as a starter. With beef we serve a slightly smaller version. When the large Yorkshire pudding first appeared on our menu they were quite novel, and in case it needs saying our puddings are not to be mistaken for the frozen varieties that are widely available. Not many make them as big and fresh as Baldwin's we always serve it with our own white onion sauce and proper gravy.

Ingredients

4 large eggs, stored at room temperature

200g strong plain white flour

750ml semi-skimmed milk

A large pinch of salt

10 tablespoons vegetable oil or beef dripping

Method

1. Place the eggs in a bowl. Gently whisk them and gradually add the flour and salt a little at a time until you have a smooth paste.
2. Gradually add the milk and continue to whisk until the mixture is the consistency of double cream.
3. Pre-heat the oven to 190˚c.
4. Put a tablespoon of oil or beef dripping into the cold baking tins (If using beef dripping place the tins in the oven to heat the fat before adding the batter). Pour 50ml of batter mix into each one.
5. Place in the oven and bake until risen and golden brown, approximately 20 minutes.
6. Serve with Baldwin's rich onion sauce and proper gravy, see page 107 for our recipes.

Hot Prawns en Cocotte

Serves 10 people

This is probably our longest-standing seafood starter, and it remains forever popular. The dish is easy to prepare on the day of your dinner party. Just allow the sauce to cool before placing over the prawns and finishing with breadcrumbs. That way you can pop them in the oven while enjoying your aperitifs and with your guests knowing your starter is under control.

Ingredients

400g cooked, skinned and trimmed prawns

220g white breadcrumbs

Large bunch chopped parsley

3 tablespoons olive oil

4 teaspoons Worcester sauce

110g grated Cheddar cheese

110g salted butter

180g plain flour

1 litre semi-skimmed milk, warmed through

1 teaspoon Coleman's English mustard

Salt and pepper to season

10 ramekins

Method

1. Take 10 ramekins, grease and place on a baking sheet.
2. Divide the prawns evenly between the ramekins, sprinkle with chopped parsley and place in the fridge.
3. For the sauce, melt the butter in a heavy-bottomed pan. Add flour and mustard to make the roux. Gradually add the warmed milk until the consistency of double cream. Add half the Cheddar cheese and salt and pepper to taste.
4. To make the topping, mix the remaining Cheddar cheese into the breadcrumbs, add a handful of chopped parsley and the Worcester sauce and 3 tablespoons of olive oil. Rub together.
5. Remove the ramekins from the fridge. Cover the prawns with the sauce, add a sprinkle of breadcrumb topping, and then bake in the oven for 20-25 minutes, at 170˚c, until golden brown and the sauce is bubbling at the edges.
6. Serve with fresh warm bread and garnish with sprig of parsley and a slice of lemon.

Jambon Persillé à la Bourgogne

A dish I always enjoyed on my wine visits to Bourgogne. Like most of the great French food its origins lie in the peasant's farmhouse.

Ingredients

6 large ham hocks

1 carrot

2 sticks celery

1 bunch of parsley

2 onions

Salt and pepper

For the vinaigrette:

3 tablespoons oil

1 tablespoon vinegar

1 shallot, finely chopped

Season to taste with
salt and pepper

You also require:

1 x 2 lb loaf tin

Method

1. Pick parsley from stalks, retain these and roughly chop the leaves. (It does not have to be small). Leave to one side.
2. Place the ham hocks and carrot, celery and onion and the stalks from the picked parsley into a large pan.
3. Cover with plenty of cold water and add salt and pepper to taste.
4. Bring to the boil on a medium heat and simmer for 4 hours until the meat is tender and falling off the bone.
5. Prepare your mould by rubbing a little oil inside the mould and lining with cling film making sure there are no holes in the cling film – the oil should make it stick to the tin.
6. When the ham is tender and falling off the bone, using a large spoon, separate all the meat onto a tray and pass the remaining liquid through a sieve into a bowl and leave to one side. Pick off all the meat and discard all the bone and gristle.
7. To arrange the dish, layer up alternately the ham, parsley and a little stock until all the tin is full. The great thing about this is that if there is too much liquid the meat will press it down and the excess liquid will spill out.
8. When the dish is cool, cover with more cling film and leave in the fridge for 24 hours to set.
9. When ready to serve turn the mixture out onto a chopping board. Remove the cling film and slice into pieces about 1.5cm thick.
10. To make the vinaigrette, finely chop the shallot, whisk together with the remaining ingredients and season to taste.
11. Serve with a summer salad and dress the leaves with a simple vinaigrette.

Famous Hopkinson's Fishcakes

Hopkinson's was a famous Sheffield fish restaurant on Rockingham Gate, just off the Moor. I was the general manager there from 1964 -1968. The Hopkinson family were on a par with Harry Ramsden's at the time, operating a chain of traditional fish and chip shops and a restaurant on Devonshire Street complete with plastic tables and chairs. My time with the Hopkinson family was a particular happy period of my life.

Ingredients

For the batter:

240g strong plain white flour

3 teaspoons of baking powder

Teaspoon of salt

Half pint of ice cold water

For the fishcakes:

6 medium potatoes, sliced 1cm thick into 48 Slices

2 large fillets of cod, skinned (350g)

3 tablespoons plain flour for dusting

Salt and pepper to season

Method

1. To make the batter, mix the salt and baking powder into the flour then slowly add the water until the consistency is such that you can thickly coat the back of a spoon. Season to taste.
2. Boil off sliced potatoes until just cooked, be very careful not to overcook the potato.
3. Take out of the water and drain well, pat dry with a clean tea towel or muslin cloth.
4. Slice medallions of cod and place between two pieces of cooked potato. Dust in flour, and roll through the batter.
5. Deep fry for 5-6 minutes in hot vegetable oil at 180˚c.
6. Take out of the hot fat and place onto a wire tray to drain off the excess fat, serve with fat chips and mushy peas.

Game Pie – Tasty Morsels from the Poachers Sack

Serves 10 people

Our game pie always includes tasty rabbit and wild boar so some may argue it is not strictly a game pie, but no one can deny the great taste whether served in small portions as an entrée or large as a main meal. It never fails to delight.

Ingredients

For the pastry:

200g butter, salted and cold

400g plain flour

2 tablespoons milk

2 eggs

Salt and pepper

For the pie filling:

1 medium onion, diced

2 medium carrots, diced

4 sticks celery, diced

4 cloves garlic, crushed

Sprig of fresh thyme or half tablespoon of dried thyme

3lb fresh mixed game meat diced into 2cm chunks (chef suggests a mixture of pheasant, rabbit, partridge, wild boar and quail)

1 medium glass red wine

2 shots brandy

2 bay leaves

1 tablespoon plain flour

500ml good fresh chicken or game stock

Salt and pepper to taste

Method

1. To make the pastry, dice the butter and place in a bowl with the flour and season. Use your hands to rub the flour and butter together until you have a sticky dough.
2. Add the egg and milk and knead till dough is firmed.
3. Cover with cling film and place in the fridge for 30 minutes rest before rolling out ready for the pie.
4. Mix the meat, red wine, thyme, garlic, brandy and bay leaves in a sealable container and season. Seal and place in the fridge for 12 hours to marinate.
5. Drain off the meat over a bowl and preserve the marinade. Discard the bay leaves.
6. Heat a little oil in a heavy bottomed pan. Fry the diced veg until soft and browning.
7. Dust the meat with flour and brown in a separate pan. Add the veg and marinade juices to the pan with a little salt and pepper to taste.
8. Add the stock and bring to the boil. When boiling, turn down the heat and simmer for two hours until the meat is tender.
9. At this stage check the consistency. If the mixture is too thin, thicken by adding some cornflour to cold water and stirring into the mix.
10. Place the pie filling into individual pie dishes, or a large dish if you prefer, and allow to cool.
11. Roll out the pastry until it is a quarter inch thick and cut to fit the pie dishes. Place the pastry on the pies and brush with a little egg wash.
12. Place in a preheated oven at 170°c for approximately 25-30 minutes until pastry is crisp and pie filling is piping hot. Serve with some fresh seasonal greens.

Partridge Bofinger

Serves 10 people

Brasserie Bofinger, on the Rue de la Bastille in Paris, is one of the oldest brasserie establishments in France. It is really a must for anyone interested in food. Bofinger is justly famous for game and seafood dishes. There is no need to book – this is a traditional brasserie where you arrive to a great welcome and fantastic food. Well worth the wait in the queue.

Ingredients

10 partridges

10 shallots

6 cloves garlic

2 pints chicken stock

4 sprigs of thyme

2 carrots

2 sticks celery

100g diced belly bacon

6 parsnips

1 pint milk

5 pears, preferably Conference

2 tablespoons olive oil

A glass of white wine

A glass of red wine

2 cloves of garlic

1 leek

1 onion

Method

1. In a frying pan, sear the partridges all round in a little oil. Remove from pan and place into a casserole dish. Remove excess fat, refresh the pan with the red wine then pour into a casserole dish.
2. Peel and chop the carrots, onions, leeks, shallots, celery and the thyme and add to the dish, along with the bacon and peeled garlic. Cover with the chicken stock and put in a pre-heated oven for 1 hour 15 minutes at 170°c.
3. Peel 5 parsnips and rough chop them, then put in a pan with the milk. Boil until soft, purée in a blender.
4. In a pan, put 2 pints of water, a glass of white wine and 2 cloves of garlic. Peel the pears and place in the pan. Poach until soft. When cooked, remove the pears from liqueur, cut in half, split and remove core. Place on a baking tray.
5. Peel the remaining parsnip, throw away the exterior peelings then continually peel round and round the parsnip to create shavings. Deep fry these in vegetable oil until crispy and golden brown. Place to one side on paper towel to drain excess fat until you are ready to garnish the dish.
6. Remove casserole dish from the oven. Transfer partridge onto a separate plate and leave to stand.
7. Drain and pour the casserole jus into a pan and place on the stove over a high heat to reduce by half. Season and skim the fat from the jus.
8. Place the pears in a warm oven or under the grill to keep warm. Do not overheat.
9. Split the partridges from the centre bone and remove flesh. Discard the bones. Place back on the tray and put them under the bottom shelf of the grill to keep warm. Be careful not to leave under too high a heat or the meat will become dry.
10. To serve the dish, use warm plates. Place a spoon of the parsnip mash onto the centre of each plate. Lay two halves of partridge up next to it and drizzle with sauce. Garnish with warm half pear and parsnip crisps.

Baldwin's Suet Treacle Pudding

Thirty years as an ever-present on the Baldwin's Omega menu. I got the original recipe from Tuckwoods where we used to serve at least 100 portions a day. It is best made in a 2lb pudding basin.

Ingredients

500g self-raising flour

Treacle to taste

1 teaspoon salt

250g suet

375ml water (approx)

250g caster sugar

Knob of unsalted butter

Method

1. Take a steamproof metal mixing bowl big enough for 10 portions of pudding, and line with butter. Put an inch depth of treacle in the bottom and rest in the fridge.

2. In another bowl, stir the suet into the flour, salt and sugar. Add sufficient water to produce a soft dropping consistency.

3. Pour the mixture into the bowl with the treacle until three quarters full. Cover well with cling film and place the bowl over a pan of boiling water or in a steamer for 1 hour 30 minutes.

4. Serve hot with proper custard.

Classic Bread and Butter Soufflé

Possibly my favourite sweet, served at many, many banquets and as light as a feather. It is best served with homemade vanilla ice cream. We love to cook it for 200 or more whilst the guests are eating their main course. Delightful served fresh and fluffy straight from the oven. Remember it is vital to preheat your oven!

Ingredients

25g sultanas

8 slices of bread, crusts removed

9 eggs

1.5 pints double cream

Half a vanilla pod

Caster sugar to taste

50g unsalted butter

Method

1. First cut the bread in half diagonally so they are triangular. Butter them and lay overlapping in an oven proof dish. Scatter the sultanas in between the bread.
2. Add the cream, egg, sugar (to your own taste) and vanilla to a bowl and whisk together. Pour the mixture over the bread and butter and bake in an preheated oven at 180°c for about 20 minutes, or until cooked in the middle.
3. Serve simply with vanilla Ice cream and fresh raspberries.

Our Famous Beef

Our Famous Beef

Right from the start we intended to make top-quality beef a mainstay of our restaurant. We made the point by naming the lunch time restaurant the Rib Room. Each morning we cook a full sirloin and served it three ways - traditional thinly cut from the joint, New York cut straight from the joint like an entrecôte steak, and Texas Dan, a double New York very thickly carved also straight from the joint. The beef is still always served with freshly-roasted potatoes, white onion sauce and proper homemade beef gravy and Yorkshire pudding.

In the early days our supplier was my good friend Harry Rowland, who ran his fondly-remembered shop JH Rowland from Sheaf Market. Harry would source his meat from farms around Penistone and West Yorkshire, using his amazing eye for good cattle and a well-honed skill for buying it on the hoof.

However, following the BSE scare and then the foot and mouth crisis the farming industry saw the introduction of passports for cattle, where each and every beast has its own passport history, is tagged and can be traced generation to generation. This has made buying good beef a lot easier, with less left to chance. But prior to that, it was essential to have the likes of Harry on your side. He was someone who knew what he was looking at.

An equally strong relationship persists with our present-day butcher Jimmy at Doug Hebdige Butchers, an associate of our old pal Philip Knowles, a leading figure in the catering trade who looked after our beef supplies for many years until retiring. Our other major beef supplier is Richard Taylor of Owen Taylor & Sons Ltd, who sources all his beef in a location close to his shop in Leabrooks, Derbyshire, which is certainly worth a visit.

One of my great pleasures is to visit Manor Farm at Palterton to renew acquaintance with Mr and Mrs Atkins, who produce much of the beef we get from Richard. Farmer Atkins is a fount of knowledge on animal husbandry. He keeps the cattle in luxurious conditions and is convinced the way to get good meat is to treat the cattle 'well and quiet'. We saw this in practice on our last visit. He spoke in a reverential whisper while showing us the cleanest barn full of cattle I've ever seen or smelt. He insists a happy beast rewards you with great meat on the table and having sampled the result, I have to say he's got something there. Most of our beef now is Limousin and Aberdeen Angus crosses with a smattering of other highland cattle.

After the farmer of course you rely on the butcher to prepare and hang the beef and I personally insist on a minimum of 25 days hanging. It's easy to check this now. Any good butcher will know the answer. And then of course it helps if you know how to cook it and we've certainly had a lot of practice. It is essential for our oven to table banqueting that we cook our beef on the evening of the function. We time it to come out of the oven to rest for approximately one hour before it heads for the dining room to be carved. It is as freshly roasted as you can get.

I don't think it's any exaggeration to say that our beef is talked about throughout the world. Take this story, relayed by my daughter Polly while she was working in the Alps for the winter.

> *'I was sitting on a lift with two clients and another unknown gentleman in Courchevel this winter. My clients asked me why I was heading back to the UK for a few days. I explained I was doing some photography for a well-known Sheffield banqueting restaurant, mentioning no names. The unknown gentleman leaned forward and barked 'Would that be Baldwin's? Fantastic Beef! I once went there with my London firm, the best beef I've ever had'. He didn't wait for my reply. We were at the top of the chairlift and he just skied off.*

Head of the Herd at Manor Farm

Baldwin's Proper Beef Gravy

Ingredients

170g beef dripping

225g plain flour

1.5 litres hot beef stock

1 onion, roughly chopped

Method

1. Roughly chop the onion into a heavy bottomed pan. Add the beef dripping and fry until the onions start to brown.
2. Add flour to make a roux and continue cooking until browning.
3. Slowly add the hot beef stock to your desired gravy consistency stirring constantly.

Mr Baldwin's Famous Onion Sauce

Serves 10 people

White onion sauce served with your Sunday joint, whatever it may be, has been a speciality of Sheffield housewives over the years. It is not to be mistaken for sad onion gravy, as served in other parts of the country.

Ingredients

2 medium sized onions, thinly diced

25g salted butter

1 litre full cream milk

50g Plain flour

Salt and pepper to taste

Method

1. Put onions and butter in a pan with a tight-fitting lid and cook slowly on a low heat until onions are cooked without colour.
2. Add the flour to make a roux, and then start adding the warmed milk slowly until it gives you a thick sauce consistency.
3. Season to taste with salt and pepper.

The Brigade

Baldwin's Kitchen

The kitchen has always been my domain. It's a love affair that started straight after I left school to become a cook. On December 22nd 1954 I started working in the kitchen at Tuckwoods restaurant on Surrey Street under the guidance of a great chef, Norman Bradley. Norman was something of a legend of the kitchens in and around Sheffield at the time. It was also at Tuckwoods where I quickly realised the importance of a first-class restaurant manager to help get the best from the kitchen. Our manager was Arthur Woolcott, a true giant of a man, who controlled an incredibly busy restaurant with both charm and guile. He knew every member of the staff at whatever level and had a marked ability to control the characteristic excesses of the chefs. My first job on getting to the kitchen on that Thursday afternoon in December was to prepare the onions for the next day's *mise en place*. In those days the bag of onions weighed 56 pounds. I had to peel and chop at least two to three bags into three different finishes; sliced, Julienne and onion rings. You could say my main qualification has been 55 years of chopping. I have never forgotten the teachings of Chef Bradley. To this day we still make all our soups freshly from scratch to the Bradley method.

Classic Chicken Stock

Ingredients

900g chicken bones
1 onion, trimmings
3 carrots
3 celery stalks
1 leek
8 sprigs of thyme
6 garlic cloves
4 pints water

Method

1. Roughly chop all the vegetables into a pan.
2. Roast the chicken bones in the oven until golden brown, for about 40 minutes.
3. Add the chicken bones, thyme and garlic to the pan and cover with the water. Bring to the boil and simmer for about 3 hours.
4. Pass through a sieve and it's ready to use.

Classic Beef Stock

Ingredients

900g beef bones
1 carrot
2 celery stalks
2 onions
8 sprigs of thyme
6 garlic cloves
4 pints of water

Method

1. Roughly chop all the vegetables into a pan.
2. Roast the beef bones in the oven until browned, for about 40 minutes.
3. Add the beef bones, thyme and garlic to the pan and cover with the water. Bring to the boil and simmer for about 3 hours.
4. Pass through a sieve and it's ready to use.

I was eventually dismissed from Tuckwoods for adding an extra week of holiday onto a trip I made cycling round Scotland with my friend Gordon (Wilf) Ramsden, an act of foolhardiness that was not appreciated by Mr Woolcott. I have to say if one of my staff were to pull the same trick they would be out on their ear too. I will always remember Tuckwoods as the place where I learned the inspiration and principles behind running a kitchen.

I am pleased to say these days I am no longer the top man in the kitchen. That role has been taken by our Head Chef Stephen Roebuck. Stephen came to me as a schoolboy at 15 some 21 years ago, He's been with us ever since. He is a young man who I liked from day one and set about training for just the role he does now so superbly well. During his training period he spent time at my dear friend Richard Shepherd's Langans brasserie in London and also had some experience at The Dorchester. He has spent many an evening dining with his wife Jane and the Baldwin's at some of the best restaurants in the land. We worked together side by side in the kitchen for 18 years or so, then for a further four years while I gradually took a step back and he has pushed on, forever improving our standards. So great is his influence that I can now think of not one item that comes through the kitchen door ready prepared by any outside agency. One recent innovation was making Baldwin's totally self-sufficient for bread production. In 2009 Stephen decided it was time to bake our own and I am now greeted by the incomparable smell of freshly-baked bread that wafts through the hallway as one arrives in the morning.

For a kitchen that often produces 1,250 meals per week we have very little refrigeration back-up. This is because we adhere to our first principle which is to buy fresh food from our local markets and suppliers and use it immediately. What we don't sell today the staff eat tomorrow. Fresh supplies arrive daily, with the single exception of meat since we observe lengthy controlled maturing times. It is really important to us that we know where our meat comes from. We make regular visits to both our suppliers and producers. The relationship a restaurateur has with his butcher and producer is one of the most important of all. I encourage Steve to make regular visits to make sure we are getting the best quality available.

Stephen and I are very proud of our kitchen brigade. They have been with us for a combined 35 years, which is quite unusual in a trade renowned for high staff turnover. The current brigade is:

> *Sam Lindsay – Sous chef, 11 years.*
> *Chris 'Chippy' Yarrow – Senior chef de partie, 12 Years.*
> *Paul Jackson, – Chef de partie, 7 Years.*
> *Chris Bettles – Junior chef de partie, 3 years.*
> *Danielle Newton – Junior chef de partie, our latest recruit and now in her 2nd year.*

Each and every one of our kitchen brigade brings to the kitchen their own specialties and personality. With the exception of Danielle all the members came straight from school. All are given opportunities to go and work in other well-known establishments to broaden their culinary education.

Chef Bradley Leek and Potato Soup

Serves 10 people

Ingredients

*4 pints of vegetable stock
(see method)*

3 large leeks

2 large potatoes

2 large onions

Salt and pepper

Method

1. Trim the skin off the leeks and onions and remove the tops.
2. Put all trimmings in a pan and cover with 4 pints of water and boil them up for 30 minutes to make a stock.
3. Pass through a sieve and it's ready to use.
4. Dice all ingredients to quarter inch pieces and place in a pan.
5. When the stock has reduced by a third add the potatoes. Bring to the boil then simmer until the potatoes thicken the soup naturally.
6. Season to taste and serve with chunky bread.

Front of House

The Front of House Staff

Baldwin's Omega would not have earned its reputation without the help and support of our staff. The business is as important to them as it is to us. They have passion and pride in their work and in the company. Some of our long-serving members of staff have become as well known to our regulars as we are. Customers like to see familiar faces they have known for years. In many cases they may recognise them as the same person who served them at their wedding, then later at their 25th wedding anniversary or even their children's weddings and birthday parties.

The current front of house team are:

Janet Wilson our general manager. Janet has worked for us since she was 15 years old. She started part time at the Anglers Rest and returned to us full time when she finished college. She has been with us for over 34 years and is an integral part of the Baldwin's Omega family.

Jamie Christian, Operations manager, has over 15 years of service and is now passing his knowledge and experience on to trainee **Jamie Williams**, who started with us last year and is set to be a key member of the management team.

Sam Sanderson, your guiding light on the telephone and at the front desk taking bookings has been with us for over 7 years.

Ian Roberts started as a DJ in 1977 and has been here ever since. He is now our night time manager and again a popular figure with our regulars. He also knows the Sheffield band scene well, which helps when we are booking our evening entertainment.

Pam, Mary and Angela are the longest serving waitresses with over 70 years of service between them. They are true Baldwin's Omega family members as many of their siblings have also passed through the building in various roles from pot washers to lay up staff. Their presence is invaluable and many of our customers agree the service would not be the same without them. Sadly, as I write, Pam's retirement is imminent so we wish her well.

'Rambo' Andy the door man you all know and love started as a DJ and moved to the door. He knows all our regulars by name as well as half the taxi drivers in Sheffield, which is only one of many reasons he's a good man to have around.

Past Members of Staff

I have to give special mention to some members of staff you may remember who have gone on to other things but for many years were key cogs in our machine.

Jeremy Plester came to us from school and worked his way up to managing the bars. He passed all his knowledge on to Jamie before he left us in 2006. He was a key member of the management team and remains a great friend of Baldwin's.

Mary Booker our beloved cook retired in 2002 after 26 years of service. Mary started as a pot washer on a temporary basis and became the mainstay of the kitchen. She was the one who kept us all sane.

Also her son, **Raymond Booker**, worked in the kitchen for many years before leaving us to run his own kitchen in Essen, Germany. He is now the head chef at one of Cheshire's most fashionable Michelin-starred restaurants, the Arkle at the Chester Grosvenor.

Mark 'the manic DJ' Clapham served us for over 17 years dishing out the tunes and an abundance of fun and energy five nights a week. He sadly left us in 2005, but leaving on a high. He was as popular as our roast beef and famous for his ridiculous dancing with the curtains, there was never a dull moment with Mark around. We owe him tremendous gratitude for all his hard work and energy.

Roy Barson was for many years our night porter. He arrived every night as we were all leaving and used to spend his nights deep cleaning the kitchens. He was a valuable member of the team who knew every inch of the building. He used to say even the resident poltergeist was friendly.

Staff Stories

Rambo Andy: "We used to have wine nights when Mr B would get on stage with a celebrity and they would try to recognise the wines. One of the speaker's wives came up to me in a panic because they had managed to lock themselves out of the house, although Howard didn't know. I found a locksmith and changed the locks while her husband was on stage. He knew nothing about it. That's what we are like here. We will do what we can to help our customers, however strange the request."

Ian Roberts: "There was a time when we introduced wireless microphones and one evening Mr B was up on stage all wired up with a transmitter in his back pocket. All was well until he came off stage and walked into the kitchen with the mike still switched on. He had forgotten about it, I don't know what he found in the kitchen, but it wasn't to his liking. His 'effing and blinding' was picked up by the mike and put through the PA system much to the amusement of the gathering in the restaurant."

Jeremy Plester: "Mr B is not PC at all, but there is a great family atmosphere at the Omega. Even after I left I'm still welcomed as part of the scene. He has a heart of gold. It's a stressful job for Mr B but if he has occasion for a cross word with the staff it is forgotten about by the next day. It lasts 10 seconds then it's all forgotten"

Janet Wilson: "There are so many stories. I can tell you at least one for every week I have worked for Mr B. Not all of them are printable but one in particular springs to mind. We were half way through serving the main course at Russ Hartley's daughter's wedding, a very fine occasion, when one of the taller waitresses commented that one of the tables seemed very low. With a closer inspection I was alarmed to see that the legs of a table, which had grandparents and other more senior guests seated at it, had lost its legs and the guests were merrily enjoying their dinner while propping up the table top with their knees. With great embarrassment I approached the table when I explained the problem a cheerful guest replied 'it's ok dear, we thought we'd had one too many sherries'.

She sees to it that I am always turned out well

Your Special Occasion
Deserves Our Attention

We've already established that consistently outstanding food and first class staff are essential in a business like ours. But there's one magic ingredient to add to the list, one that truly makes someone's event special and memorable.

It's the personal touches and the presentation the customers notice the most. Although our business is large-scale catering, we strive to make the client feel as though they, and their event, are the most important we've ever handled.

To achieve this, we have a secret weapon in our armoury – it's called Pauline. While training with British Transport Hotels in the 1960s, she worked in some big hotels including The North British Hotel, Edinburgh (now the Balmoral), Turnberry, Gleneagles and finally the Royal Victoria Hotel in Sheffield. Although Pauline loved her time in these establishments she's never been fond of anything corporate and prefers the more personal service of smaller hotels. Our service is just as personal because we keep everything in-house, from the interior design, to the food and table presentation. Pauline has always done our own flowers and table decorations and we see it as a service that all customers deserve without extra charge. It's these little personal touches that make each event unique. From funky menu cards to balloons, we do it all, unless requested otherwise by our clients.

A Birthday Lunch For Pat

Saturday 11th July 2009

MENU

AMUSE BOUCHE

SWANAGE PLATTER
Scallops, Sea Bass & Lobster Sauce

LOIN OF KINGSBRIDGE DEVONSHIRE LAMB
Apricot Farci & Vegetables of The Moment

CAVENDISH CRÈME BRULEE
with Summer Berries

ASSIETTE DU FROMAGE LE NORTON
Baked Fig, Goats Cheese & Walnut

COFFEE & SWEETMEATS

Meet the Khazi King

Photograph: Roger Nadal

TO Baldwin's Omega to spend a penny with restaurateur and bon viveur David Baldwin, who has just won the best restaurant toilet category in the Loo of the Year Awards.

King of the khazi David has spent more pennies than most of us – eight million, to be exact – on his new space-age toilets.

Walk into the gents at his banqueting suite off Psalter Lane, Sheffield, and prepare to be amazed.

You will marvel at the chequered tile floor, gawp at the stainless steel 'ice cream' cone

❝ The toilets are so hi-tech I'm thinking of giving customers lessons

DAVID BALDWIN

urinals, and thrill to the moulded glass washbasins with their push button taps, set on enormous coiled steel springs.

A chap here needs to be confi-

dent of his aim when he points Percy at the porcelain. The curvature of the urinals gives a convex rather than concave effect. It's like tinkling on a dome. Rather disconcerting!

The ladies loo is even swisher with the vanity units made out of one large piece of moulded glass. Both toilets have glass tiles and walls with a champagne glass and bubbles motif.

"The toilets are so hi-tech I'm thinking of giving customers lessons," chuckles David. Not everyone has worked out that to empty the washbasin you swivel the plug with your finger.

He visited two countries in his search for fittings. "I saw the WC cubicles in a magazine and traced them to Germany only to be told their English agents were Sissons of Chesterfield."

They also made the cone-shaped urinals. He went to a factory in Italy to find the sinks.

Glass tiles come from Sheffield as do the urinal splashbacks, on which he has posted leaflets of forthcoming events. "I did put pages from the Green 'Un up but this is not a good season," he cracks.

Customers have been impressed. One woman declared the ladies to look like "the Titanic meets Ikea."

Another woman who had popped in to powder her nose complained to the doorman that she had found a man in the loo.

"Well, he's a hairdresser," explained the doorman.

"Oh, that's all right then," said the woman.

"She seemed quite happy by the explanation," laughs David.

Following the extensive refurbishment of our toilets by my son David's firm, Structural Interiors, we won the Restaurant Loo of the Year

Newspaper article reproduced with kind permission from Sheffield Newspapers Ltd.

Photographs reproduced with kind permission from Structural Interiors Ltd.
www.structuralinteriors.co.uk

Meet the Khazi King

Every job has its essential tasks that the boss has to deal with personally. Ours is eating out in other top-quality restaurants. It might sound like a good excuse for a jolly – and it's undeniably something we enjoy – but there is a serious purpose in it all. It is important to see what the trends are and constantly push for improvement in all areas of the business. Eating out has been the best source of research for us.

For example, it was during a visit to London in the mid 1990s that I decided, while sitting on one of Conran's loos, that we should modernise ours. Pauline had been pushing for us to smarten up the building to keep the younger clientelle coming through the door, but it's always difficult to get the balance right. In the case of the toilets however, we could be as avant garde as we liked – after all, whatever we did would not affect the operation of the restaurant. Impetuous as ever, we chose the wash hand basins that weekend in a shop on Old Brompton Road and the rest of the design followed naturally with the help from my son David's firm Structural Interiors. To our delight we won 'Restaurant Loo of the Year' in 1999, beating the very same Conran restaurant whose loo I had sat on when we embarked on the scheme. It's hard to believe this was over 10 years ago now.

The Restaurant Association

Of course, these visits to other restaurants create inspiration about more than just the looks. We have always been great believers in educating ourselves and our staff with regular trips to other restaurants both at home and abroad. During a recent visit to Beaune, chef and I had the pleasure of visiting Loiseau des Vignes, a Michelin-starred establishment where they have a choice of over 60 wines, all kept in perfect condition and temperature – quite remarkable. They only serve wines by the glass to ensure you get the correct one to complement your meal. Here we tasted the best soufflé we'd ever had and also the best soup. It was a truly magnificent meal which no doubt will be recreated at a banquet in the near future. Our luncheon à la carte menu already plays host to some of the dishes we tried and, naturally, the wines.

Pauline and I have been members of the The Restaurant Association since the Anglers days in the late seventies. It has been of great benefit to us over the years, giving us the chance to meet other people in the business. The association gives fantastic freedom to discuss your business and ideas with others whose are not based in the same immediate area and so are not in direct competition. It has been a great learning experience over the years. We have made many good friends and it has also helped the business keep on progressing in both quality and style. In more recent years I have been more involved with the association and in 2008 I became its president, a role I loved fulfilling until I recently stepped down. Pauline and I continue to be active members as it is so important for the business. My dear friend Gordon Clark, who I have worked with for many years, has kindly summed up my time as a committee member and chairman. I am most grateful to him and the association for the support they have given us over the years.

George David Baldwin

LICENSED TO SELL ANY INTOXICATING LIQUOR
FOR CONSUMPTION ON THE PREMISES
& FOR PUBLIC MUSIC SINGING & DANCING

Thank You Mr. President

Thank You, Mr President

My name is Gordon Clark and for the last 17 years I have been the Northern Director of The Restaurant Association, the national trade body for the hospitality industry. It was my job not only to know our members, but to work with them to make sure they are up to date with new legislation and receive all the benefits of membership.

The profile of association members ranges from very small bistros run by the chef and partner, to the top restaurants in the country's largest and best-known hotels such as The Savoy or The Dorchester – and in the north, the very popular Midland Hotel in Manchester. I worked with them all. Some were more co-operative than others, but generally speaking, they were all pleased to be members of a trade body that promoted quality and skills within the hospitality industry.

Meeting the Man

Some restaurateurs had been members long before I came on the scene in 1993. I clearly remember the day during my first year when I headed over the Snake Pass for Sheffield to introduce myself to one of the longest-serving members of the association, David Baldwin, who had been a member since the early eighties.

I had heard many descriptions about David. Some were quite intimidating. Big and brash, doesn't suffer fools gladly, calls a spade a spade, don't give him any waffle… all this information was passed on to me by those who knew David, so I was to say the least, a little apprehensive when I approached Baldwin's Omega for the first time.

I arrived at a large banqueting restaurant with a vast car park. I was most impressed. I asked for David at reception. "Sorry he's not in yet, take a seat and I'll get you a coffee. He will be here soon." Everybody seemed very friendly.

So I sat and waited, within a few minutes he arrived. I could hear this loud voice as he arrived in the building and came towards where I was waiting. " Nar-then Clarky. Did tha' have a good trip over?" – I knew from that minute we would get on.

He was what I call a 'no bullshit man' none of this 'my food's better than his food' rubbish. It was obvious he cared deeply about training his staff and producing quality food for his customers, without pretending to be some snooty French-trained Michelin-starred chef. In fact for lunch we had roast beef and Yorkshire pudding cooked to perfection. We had a great first meeting that day and I was soon to be a regular visitor to the Omega.

The Party Years

Over the following years, during the late nineties and early millennium I worked closely with David, who was always there to support any ideas for getting members together. It was a time when we held a lot of meetings with celebrity guest speakers and David knew them all. One call from the 'Big Un' as he was then known and they would be there to support us in the north. The top men such as Roy Ackerman, Richard Shepherd, Anthony Worrall-Thompson, Raymond Blanc, Paul Heathcote, Brian Turner, Terry Laybourne and Nigel Haworth and Craig Barcroft from Northcote, all freely gave up their time to talk to members.

By now the northern section of The Restaurant Association was working well thanks to the support of a nucleus of members including David, who backed all our activities. David and Pauline were very supportive when we started a Northern Golf Day. This was closely followed by an annual North v South golf competition and we held our Christmas party at the Omega on a number of occasions.

Recognition

All this activity didn't go unnoticed, and although he already sat on The Restaurant Association committee, the other committee members saw his willingness to get involved and his enthusiasm to communicate with members. So many of them looked up to David as a senior committee member.

The committee voted David vice-chairman until November 2005, at which time he would become chairman. He was delighted. He had lots of plans to improve things for the members. The first thing he did was to take the Young Chef/Young Waiter awards to a higher level. This national competition had been running for almost 20 years, but David gave it some momentum and arranged through his contacts that the final presentation of the winners would be made in the Houses of Parliament by a minister, a real incentive for any youngster entering the hospitality industry.

It's hard to describe the time and effort David put in as chairman but it was certainly way in excess of what was expected. He was invited to all types of launches and functions, sat on a variety of committees – mostly at his own expense – and it certainly was a workload he could do without. But he loved it. He can't help himself – he just loves helping people and the members certainly appreciated him as a very active chairman.

During his two years in office we developed a slightly different style of communicating with members. Out went the big meetings and in came the smaller gatherings for about 20 people where members could have their say and discuss things in detail. The Chairman's Lunches were born. We held four or five lunches a year in all of the major northern cities. David hosted every meeting, without payment and in addition to his normal work of running the Omega.

Presidential Years

After two years as chairman his period of office was over and he was replaced by Bob Walton MBE in November 2008. The mere fact that David had been so active for the last two years put a lot of pressure on the new chairman. He was left wondering how to follow such an act.

The answer was simple – appoint David as president for the next two years and ask him to carry on with all the lunches. Members would also be encouraged to continue to contact him for help and advice.

The question was, would Pauline agree to David putting in all those extra hours and not having him around at the Omega? I don't know what was said, but at the end of the day David accepted the presidency. I think that conversation cleared the air and since then I'm sure they have the blend of Omega work and Restaurant Association duties spot on. I can tell you that the last couple of years have been an absolute joy, working with David hosting the President's Lunches around the country. Unfortunately his time as president came to an end during 2010.

Throughout their time in business, especially at the Omega, David and Pauline have made many friends. They also made many good friends within the Association. For my part, during my 17 years at the Association I have met some really nice people, who will remain friends, but the one who stands out from all the people I have met is Big David Baldwin and his wife Pauline – it's been a privilege.

"Ooph... summat else that soup, gob-smacking flavour!"
Mr B's first taste of the Vichyssoise at Loiseau des Vignes, Beaune

Wines My Way

Château Lascombes 1992-ish

Wines My Way

Beer, G&T or perhaps port and lemon. There was a time when nearly every bar order featured at least one of this holy trinity. If you wanted wine, communion was your best bet.

Even then, in the days long before supermarket shelves were bulging with the stuff, I always felt wine had an ever more important role to play in the licensed trade. Luckily for me, I was to be handed the opportunity to play my part in the transformation.

In my early days at The Wheatsheaf as a publican, my employers Tetley's also owned Grants of St. James's wine company. Luckily, they were the very first company to offer wine training for managers and bar staff. The lengths they went to included taking over a hotel in Otley, where they staged residential courses on the general running of a public house and newly-emerging wines. I was already an enthusiast about wines from my earlier career and I jumped at the opportunity to do my intermediate wine exam.

Anyone with memories of the seventies will probably recall Grants of St James's Tetley wines on the shelves under the name of Nicolas, great wines from France which are still sold throughout France and the Nicolas shop in London. However it was during my time at the Anglers Rest in Bamford that I was really able to indulge myself with an extensive list and improve my knowledge with the help of the wines and spirits company Taplows. It was at the Anglers that we sold thousands of bottles of *Hirondelle a vin ordinaire* which was ostensibly Austrian wine brought to Britain by Heinz Barron. However the lid was blown on the origins of the wines by a Sunday

Times writer who noticed more of the wine was sold in the UK than was actually produced in the whole of Austria and the bubble burst.

It turned out to be as big a sham as the Barron, but just like the Barron, it gave a great deal of pleasure.

I suppose you could say my wine philosophy is strictly based on the fact that I like it. But I suppose my tastes are not that of the average wine buff. For a start I have always had a passion for Rosé wines, not something many men of my size would confess to. Many of my friends think I am quite crazy in my passion for pink. When I order Mateus Rosé in an Indian restaurant, I tell them curry without Rosé is like a ship without a sail. The owner of my favourite Sheffield Indian restaurant, The Ashoka on Ecclesall Road, now frowns at having Mateus Rosé on the wine list, but the waiter, young Cameron, keeps me the odd bottle or two in an out of the way fridge.

The great Rosé wines of the world come from Provence in France and many of them now command high prices, including my favourite Domaine D'Ott, in its famous skittle shaped bottle. So over the years I have sourced other Rosés from around the world. That is why Baldwin's has had up to 10 varieties of Rosé on its wine list, and they have become a major part of our sales. It's pleasing that a personal taste like this has found wider favour, in the same way that people would join me at the bar as I polished off copious quantities of Noilly Prat at the bar, and try what it has to be said, is an acquired taste.

I have no particular likes or dislikes, but on one thing I am insistent. Some 15 years or so ago I was with my late friend Tearle Phelan on a Sunday lunchtime in what was then our beloved local, the Derwent Inn at Bamford. We made a pact and solemnly declared that henceforth we were "too old to drink crap". Indeed, up until his untimely death we made a habit of drinking only the very best. Cheers Tearle!

Around 1974, I met Eddie Legard, an ex-professional cricketer who worked for Bass Taplows wine shippers in Huddersfield as stock controller. He was a veritable fount of knowledge on wines, having spent many rainy days in pavilions reading about it and supping more than a drop. I persuaded him to apply for a wine adviser's job with the brewery. He landed the job and his career and our friendship flourished. He has helped me a great deal over the years. I still occasionally enjoy a good lunch with him and his lovely wife Mari.

When we started the Omega it was the first time we had been free to buy our wines where and when we wanted. Today our list is a long reflection of the relationships with winemakers, producers and agents we have built up over the years around the world. Over time we have made many trips, visiting many of the great vineyards of Europe and Australia. Stalwart members of these expeditions included Dick and Faith Gilbert and Barry and Val Wheat. In all there were around 20 trips. Many of them became legendary, particularly amongst the members of Sickleholme Golf Club. Our current wine list is a result of 30 years of research and tasting.

Mr B, Mr Wheat & Mr Gilbert – a working lunch in Rhône

I've seen many changes in tastes over the years. Among the biggest shifts has been the demise of German wines in the restaurant trade. I remember when 10 per cent of our sales were accounted for by Liebfraumilch and Niersteiner. We used to sell six bottles of white for every three reds. Nowadays it's about 50/50. Taste in aperitifs has changed too. We used to sell lots of gin and tonic and every week got through six bottles of Noilly Prat – the proper vermouth for Martini cocktails. Now people seem to like wine or lager before dinner now.

The Baldwin's Wine Selection

All the wines on our list have been personally chosen by me and my team. A good wine knowledge is really important for the staff and we make great efforts to advance their education so we can bring our clients a great variety of choice and, above all, quality wines and value for money.

Champagnes

Our champagne list is headed by Champagne Baldwin along with its sister Baldwin Selection du Patron Rosé. We have had our own label for 20 years or more. It comes from Ellner of Epernay in the heart of the Champagne region. I am particularly proud of it because our label is registered with the Champagne authorities and we have our own unique domain number. It is no longer possible to achieve this. I am forever grateful to John Townend of The House of Townend wine merchants who helped us secure our own label as well as continuing supplies. We have a great selection of other Champagnes including products from Bollinger, with whom we enjoy a close relationship.

French Wines

I enjoy wines from the new world, indeed from across the world. But in my view French wines are still the finest and so the restaurant list carries a large selection of the wines of France. Recently chef and I had a chance to sample some of the country's finest during a most interesting visit to Beaune in Burgundy, where we visited some of our favourite winemakers.

Chanson Père & Fils

I was first introduced to Chanson wines in the 1970s by Victor Grainger of Grainger Wines, who along with his brother ran a very fine wine merchants in Sheffield. The house of Chanson Père & Fils was established some 250 years ago, but this French wine growing company lost its way and faded in the late 1970s. But since being bought by the Bollinger family some 10 years ago Chanson has returned to its old traditional methods. Bollinger have put vast amounts of money into Chanson and in particular into the *terroir* (earth), the most important part of the vineyard. Without good soil and skilful cultivation you cannot produce great vines. Good vines will blossom and yield superb fruit and of course grand wine. We have several of Chanson's classic wines on our list.

My personal choice is *Viré-Clessé Chanson 2006*, a fine example of Chardonnay from the Mâconnais region of Burgundy. A delight with fish or seafood or just to quaff. A zingy, long, flinty after taste. Near perfect.

Philippe Dufouleur – Domaine Loïs Dufouleur

Also from Burgundy is a house with which we have a particular relationship – the small boutique grower Philippe Dufouleur from the Domaine Loïs Dufouleur. We were introduced to Philippe by my old pal Robert Rusby at Hallamshire Wine in Sheffield and since then I have enjoyed many visits to Philippe. Over the years he has taught me a great deal about Burgundy and wine in general.

I highly recommend visiting Beaune. It is a beautiful historic city where you can't fail to discover something new with every visit. Phillipe has a quite magnificent home set within his gardens and beside his cellars. It is a truly serene location right in the centre of Beaune. In sharp contrast to the larger wine maker Chanson, which produce in excess of 900,000 bottles of wine per year, Philippe accounts for only 30,000 bottles. You can almost taste the love and attention he and his family put into the vines with every glass. I never make a visit to Beaune without dropping in to see my friend and find out how the recent harvest is maturing. Philippe's wines are all from the Beaune area, and he produces some of the finest red Burgundy's available, together with some rather good whites.

My personal choice: *Loïs Dufouleur Beaune Clos Du Dessus Des Marconnets 2003*. A classic example of Pinot noir from Philippe Dufouleur, a small producer but a perfectionist. Just right with Baldwin's beef or roast lamb. Save a drop to go with your Stilton – perfection.

Bourgogne is of course not the only region of France making fine wines. I am very fond of whites from the Loire, reds from Rhône and the more spicy wines from the Alsace. We also stock the mighty Bordeaux (clarets) that are still popular, although many of the historic houses of the region have been priced out of the restaurant market. It is still possible with the help from our merchant friends, such as the House of Townend and Chris Ward at Penistone Court Wines, to source very good value clarets from many of the smaller and less pompous growers of the region. However France no longer dominates the world wine market and I have great passion for Spanish wines.

Le Belle Les Jardins de Loïs, Beaune

Spanish Wines

I have made many visits to the Spanish wine regions, but my beloved Rioja is the one I hold in greatest affection. Grupo Faustino have several vineyards and labels and our wine list features almost all of their wines. Foremost among them is my particular favourite, Faustino I Rioja Gran Reserva. A Rioja that is true to its roots, a complex wine which needs to be taken with food and goes especially well with Baldwin's beef. There is little I can think of more satisfying than a large glass alongside a plate of the finest beef.

Another great Faustino to try and featured on our menu is Faustino V Blanco Sin Crianza, a white wine with no oak. I not only enjoy this wine but I am proud of it. It is made entirely from the historic white grape of Spain, Viura. Until recently, like almost all Spanish wines, this one was finished with oak. During a tasting trip with Pauline I suggested to the wine makers of Faustino that they could try to make it without the oak – and they did!

The difference is quite staggering. It is now a great zingy wine, lovely to drink in the sunshine with all fish and white meats. Try it, you'll like it. We also stock rosé wines from Faustino.

A tasting (drinking) with Mr Manu Muga himself

My other Spanish favourite is of course the Bodegas Muga, another great maker of the area. It's been the venue for many visits, most recently with my daughter and her boyfriend Lee in May 2010, Polly was clearly impressed:

I have been extremely lucky over the years to visit some of the finest vineyards in Europe with my parents and although I have some knowledge I am in no way an authority on wines. However, I base my selection of personal favourites around particular grape varieties. It's intriguing to discover the variation in styles that different makers create from those same grapes.

I have long been a fan of Muga Rosé and often enjoy a glass or two with my Dad so I was excited to make this, my first visit to Rioja and Bodega Muga. It adds a different dimension of enjoyment when the opportunity arises to see how a familiar wine is made. I have never been as impressed with an operation as I was with Muga. As an advocate for tradition, and traditional ways, I was pleased to see how the house operates. Our hosts Mr Manu Muga and Mr Jesus Vigue have a charming way of explaining the production processes.

'It's all about the timing. Imagine you have a red grape and you crush it between two fingers. You can make white wine out of the fruit. If you add the skin to the mixture and macerate it for 12 hours before removing the skin you make a rosé. If you left the skin for 12 weeks you would get a red'

That's winemaking explained rather well in one paragraph.

It was not just our host's manner of speaking that impressed me. The whole ethos of Muga is based around family traditions that have been in place since 1932. At present the winery is located in a beautiful mansion at Haro in the heart of Rioja. There are no modern methods, nor any stainless steel in sight. Fermentation and maceration are carried out in wooden vats and barrels made in their own cooperage, the only one of its kind in Rioja. They also differ from other houses in using the time-honoured gravity based racking and preferring egg whites for clarification of their red wines.

I came face to face with tradition when I entered the huge cellar crammed with barrels. There, intent on his work, was one of the few men whose sole task was to control the fermentation by hand, turning the barrels and removing any unwanted sediment without the use of any modern gadgets. It's an arduous task, carried out with love, great care and dedication.

I was also impressed by the fact that nothing is wasted. After being separated from the whites, the egg yolks are sold to the local bakery to make little cakes. Likewise the dust and chippings from the cooperage are bound together to make kindling for fires and sold at local markets. It's a unique cottage industry that is both inspiring and remarkable.

In true Baldwin style we were treated to breakfast and a tasting with Mr Muga, which truth be told, was more drinking than tasting. We accounted for several bottles of Mr Muga's own choosing, and he introduced me to his wonderfully drinkable reds while Dad tried to persuade Mr Muga that making a magnum of Muga Rosado would be a "marvellous idea". I do hope he managed to convince him as one bottle is rarely enough!

Polly A. Baldwin

We have wines from many other regions of Spain and the rest of Europe, including Austria. There are too many to mention by name but each and every wine on the list comes with my personal recommendation.

I remember one particular trip we made to Austria back in 2000. I liked one vintage so much that I purchased the entire stock. I thought the diners at the restaurant would find the name 'Gruner Veltliner 1997 Alt Reben Anton Wober Wrinverte' a bit of a mouthful so I had the whole lot relabelled 'Brincliffe'.

Diners at Baldwin's can take added assurance from the fact that we carry a selection from one of our newer suppliers, Corney and Barrow. An independent wine merchant of high repute who enjoy the patronage of the royal family among others. They were established in 1780, but have quite a new relationship with Baldwin's. Our offering from them is small but quite comprehensive. When in London, a visit to one of the Corney and Barrow wine bars is a must.

We pride ourselves on an unpretentious approach to wines, if diners are seeking advice on which wine to choose we are more than pleased to give recommendations.

A super visit to Joseph Drouhin

With Mr & Mrs Brown in Milawa, Western Australia

Brown Brothers Wines
Dinner

King Valley Pinot Noir & Chardonnay NV

1999 Verdelho

1999 Late Harvested Muscat

1996 Nebbiolo

1997 Barbera

1999 Orange Muscat & Flora

1994 Limited Release F.R Cabernet Shiraz

Surprise liqueur

Baldwins
OMEGA

Baldwins
Tuesday 10th October 2000

Loch Fynne Smoked Salmon Canapés

Chargrilled Sea Bass and Sardine Salad
Chargrilled fresh fillets on frisee lettuce and fresh herb leaves with basil dressing

Yorkshire Hors D'Oeuvre
A mini Yorkshire pudding with foie gras and caramelised onions

Pasta Linguini
Pasta with sun blush tomato, olive flesh and pesto

Assiette of New Seasons Lamb - Baldwin
A delicate selection of lamb flavours with a timbale of
minted couscous and Milawa mustard sauce

Chocolate Orange Pudding
A steamed chocoholics delight to die for

Milawa Cheese with Roast Walnuts
from David Brown at the Milawa cheese factory

Coffee and Friends

With Chris Ward from Penistone Wines

New World Wines

I never quite joined the exodus to the new world wines but no one can doubt their amazing success over the last few years. The phenomenal rise in the volume of wines produced in Chile, along with the outstanding quality, has created a remarkable success story. Our list reflects this with a very good cross-section of Chileans. From Australia we feature mainly Brown Brothers, whom we had the pleasure of visiting with Chris Ward from Penistone Wines. Indeed we stayed with the Brown family at their wonderful home base of Milawa in Western Australia. If you are in Melbourne or Sydney it is quite an easy drive. Brown Brothers run a gourmet restaurant at their vineyards, and enjoy a reputation as pioneers of matching food and wine. Our very first wine night was inspired by our visit to Brown Brothers and we were lucky in 2001 to have Ross Brown, the chairman of the company, honour us with a visit to work with our kitchen and produce a memorable wine night, with food that did justice to their excellent wines.

Wine Nights

When we host one of our spectacular wine dinners, we always work closely with the winemakers on the proposed menu, taking their advice on matching the wines to the food – and sometimes vice versa. Among the most outstanding dinners was the Joseph Drouhin event, remembered for the presence of the very dashing young Christian Drouhin who stayed and danced the night away with the ladies.

Baldwin's House Selection

Without doubt our biggest selling wine is the Patron de Baldwin which unsurprisingly comes from France. It is our own blend and label and I take great pleasure in visiting the supplier every now and then with John Townend to re-blend the wines to my liking.

We recently re-blended our ever popular house selection using fresh wines from the 2006 vintage. The white still comes from the Montpellier region using Ugni-Blanc and Colombard grapes, which benefit from the strong Mediterranean influences.

Baldwin's Rouge is grown near Pau in the Pyrenees and the grapes enjoy a microclimate of warm days and cool nights. We use Syrah, Carignan and Merlot grapes, which harmonise to create a smooth easy drinking red. All the wines are young, fruity and naturally great with food.

I honestly believe the most important wines on the list are the house recommended wines, including our own Champagne. We also have the Don Darias range from Spain and our 'pure' house wines from The House of Townend. I feel it's important to have different house wines available so that the client has a good choice.

An up to date wine list is always available on our website at www.baldwinsomega.com

My old pal John Mitchell runs what is without doubt the finest wine shop in Sheffield, Mitchells Wines at Meadowhead. I recommend you have a visit there to select your wines for that all-important dinner party. John, along with his wife Lynda, is always great company and one of life's real pleasures is sitting down to dinner with the two of them. He has recently done a two-year spell as President of the Yorkshire Wines and Spirits Society so really knows his stuff. By the way if your man likes cigars, Meadowhead is the place to go for a fine selection – quite a rarity these days.

Listening and laughing with "The Big 'Un"

Functions – A Social History

The process of making this book has been interesting in many ways. We still have all our business diaries and many of our menus from our very first opening in 1981 to present day. It is fascinating to see how the business has changed over the years, and the differences between the clientele we had then and the kind of food we served, not to mention some of the prices. How does £6 per head for five courses, wine and dancing to a live band sound? That was the going rate in 1984, if only that was possible nowadays.

The function – a reflection of the times

What do you call a roomful of 150 people? Some might say a crowd. We beg to differ. In our way of thinking, they're 150 individuals.

We approach everything we do with one principle in mind – that what is served to a large gathering should be no different from what a table for four would expect. We believe customers should not be surprised they had outstanding food and service at a banquet. That's despite the fact that barely a day passes without someone commenting that the food was of a standard indistinguishable from what they would enjoy on their night out at a quality restaurant.

We may hear that often, but we don't tire of it as it means we must be doing our job right.

And yet, back at the beginning, it actually took a couple of years for people to trust us with their very special occasions such as weddings and birthdays. The result was that in the early days we did a lot of company functions. The Baldwin's Omega diaries from 1981 onwards show an amazing picture of social change in Sheffield. The lion's share of functions from our first year were from two groups that don't appear at all in the diaries of today. The first of these was the sports and social clubs associated with large firms. Today most work functions are paid for by the firm and are predominantly an annual event, but in those days employees paid for their own tickets. Each company's social club would organise an annual night out, yet this sort of function was almost extinct ten years later. The other group was the annual bash from various pubs. A lot of these were very large, attracting up to 260 or 300 and were organised by the landlord and landlady of the locals. They came from all over the city... The Crown at Totley, The Forty Foot at Hillsborough, The Old Harrow at Grenoside and many more.

Sadly, just like the company events, these celebrations are now consigned to the past. I often wonder if that is due to the decline of the traditional landlord and landlady, who used to enjoy having a social gathering to foster a community spirit among their customers.

So much for the bigger functions. Smaller events were – and still are – held by groups such as, fishing clubs, darts clubs and the like.

From our second year onwards we saw the growth in clubs and associations for professionals. We had the support of the Vulcan Rotary Club from the beginning, most of whose original members became great friends and life long devotees. These were now joined by Abbeydale Rotary and various Round Tables, 41 clubs and tangents whose area meetings in those days attracted around 200 and were noted for always being a lively event.

The mid-eighties were a great era of growth for the country as a whole, and this coincided with a growing taste for finer foods and a good night out. It was also a time when we saw a relatively new phenomenon, one which is still much in demand today. The charity function had arrived.

GRAND CHARITY BALL

The CHRIS FUND acknowledges with warm thanks the generous contributions made to this evening by the following:

Al Castings Ltd.
Arkote Ltd.
Buck & Hickman Ltd.
Arthur Edge & Co. Ltd.
T. C. Harrison PLC
John Heath Funeral
Directors Ltd.
Jacobs Manufacturing Ltd.
Kenning Car Hire Ltd.
KSR International Ltd.

Arthur Lee PLC
Neill Tools Ltd.
Peat, Marwick & Mitchell
Post House Hotels Ltd.
Presto Tools Ltd.
Stanley Tools Ltd.
Sugg Sport Ltd.
The Wine Schoppen
Woodcock Travel Ltd.

MARDI GRAS MENU

New Orleans Cocktail

Mardi Gras Soup

Chilli Con Carne

Honey Baked Chicken

A Selection of Vegetables

Banana Foster

Coffee and Mints

HELP THE CHRIS FUND?

The **CHRIS FUND** raises money to be used by the medical staff at the Sheffield Children's Hospital on a variety of research projects. Recent examples have been an extension to the Ryegate Annexe for the assessment of handicapped children, a programme to equip health visitors with weighing scales, to help prevent cot deaths, and research into digestive problems (won't go into this one while you're eating your dinner!)

We particularly welcome help from any individual or organisation who feels that they would like to organise some event to raise money for us, whether on a large or small scale.

Please contact:
Barbara Barr on Sheffield 364209 or Peter Ford on Sheffield 360417

The very first charity function was organised by Jane Laver for Cherry Tree Children's Homes on 24th September 1982. Our most longstanding prestigious do of the year is Sheffield Children's Hospital Ball (Chris Fund Charity Ball) which since 1984 has always been on the first Saturday in March. Now known as the Daffodil Ball, it was originally organised by Peter Ford and Jackie Paramour. We served a Mardi Gras themed menu which we believe was the first in a long line of themed nights at Baldwin's. It was taken over in the 1990s by Nigel Worthington of Sheffield Wednesday fame, along with wife Sandra, before passing into the stewardship of Jean and David Fyfe. It has helped raised the charity tens of thousands of pound over the years.

Other highlights of the charity season that have been with us since the mid-nineties are the St Luke's Ball on the last Saturday of September, first booked by Linda Burns and lately by Dick Atkinson, the author of that fine opus 'Ode to Baldwin's' at the beginning of this book. Sheffield Animal Hospital Ball organised by Kath Whitlam has been with us through three decades too. However the biggest do we have ever held in terms of fund-raising came in 2005 when Garry Scotting of Sheffield VW Audi and team organised a fund raising evening and charity auction, for the national appeal to help tsunami victims. Everybody involved gave their time and expertise for free including the musicians, and Baldwin's donated all the ticket money to the charity. I was privileged to be auctioneer that evening. More than £100,000 was raised in one evening, a truly magnificent figure from just 264 guests with very generous pockets!

From the mid-eighties onwards we saw a steady increase in bookings from the more affluent areas of Sheffield. Manufacturing was a different story, as this was the time of widespread closures. Indeed the only manufacturing firms that have supported us from the beginning and are still with us today, are the first-ever firm to book an event in 1981, George Robson and Co, and Newburgh Engineering, who have been ever-present since 1982.

At this time people were moving away from their firm's sports and social clubs and joining more upmarket private clubs. We started to pick up the new functions of the annual sports clubs social dinner dances. There is a long list of sports clubs that began to frequent Baldwin's, and who are still to be seen there today. They include Sickleholme Golf Club, Sheffield Casual Cricket club, Collegiate and Parkhead Cricket Clubs, Sheffield and Hallam football clubs, Sheffield Hockey Club, Sheffield Cricket Lovers Association, Tigers Rugby Club, Sheffield Eagles Rugby Club and, in the early nineties, Hallamshire Tennis Club.

A last night at the Prom

DJs and posh frocks help say goodbye to schooldays

WE'VE just come to the end of Sheffield's school Proms when sixth formers leaving for university say goodbye to their schooldays with a formal black tie dinner and dance.

Their parents, many of whom grew up in the era of flower power when the accepted rig-out was long hair and jeans, have been looking on bemusedly at their penguined sons, the very model of conformity.

Celebrating in style doesn't come cheap. Hiring a suit costs from £26, says Anne Johnson at Philip Johnson's at Banner Cross. "The full package, with shirt, tie and cummerbund, is £38. Last Tuesday we had the High Storrs prom and we did 28 outfits, all in the smaller sizes."

Kitted out, a High Storrs student would then have paid £15 for his ticket at Baldwin's Omega which bought a dinner of cream of vegetable soup, chicken and profiteroles, followed by a disco.

Proms are a relatively new phenomenon in the last five or six years and Baldwin's claims to be the venue for all the schools but one, Birkdale. Where the idea sprang from no one is sure but it could have been the influence of American high school

movies which always feature proms.

Some 298 pupils celebrated High Storrs Prom last Tuesday, followed by 244 from Notre Dame on the Thursday.

Baldwin's manager Janet Wilson says the proms bring welcome midweek business. "You get some of the lads wearing dinner jackets with a pair of trainers because they don't have a proper pair of shoes. And sometimes they club together to hire a stretch limo.

"On the whole they are very well behaved. At first we were unsure what to expect. Their schools tell them if they don't behave it will spoil it for future years."

Notre Dame doesn't have a prom but a ball. Dave Haswell, assistant head of the Sixth, says it has been going for at least nine years (when it was held at the City Hall) so the school can lay claim to being one of the first.

And it's not all disco dancing. "Someone comes in to teach the students how to ballroom dance in the weeks before the ball," he says.

"The dress codes the kids practice are brilliant. They go to great lengths to get posh frocks and hire suits."

You get some of the lads wearing dinner jackets with a pair of trainers because they don't have a proper pair of shoes. And sometimes they club together to hire a stretch limo

It seems that changing fashion hasn't diminished interest in these sports much since the eighties and we are pleased to see they all still turn out in healthy numbers to their annual dinners. Barlow Hunt Ball has been another long-standing date in the social calendar always taking place on the last Saturday in January, since 1989. The first hunt ball was organised by Gail Dunn and Avril Turner. The menu was Terrine Baldwin, Game Soup, Topside of Beef and Yorkshire pudding, Raspberry Meringue Gâteau followed by cheese and coffee, all for a very reasonable £10.75 including balloons on the tables and a disco.

The diaries spanning the time from the nineties through to the noughties reflect the economic climate of Sheffield. It's possible to see the rise of both educational and medical.

School Proms came to our shores in the nineties and have proven popular ever since.
Reproduced with kind permission from Sheffield Newspapers Ltd.

During the 30 years of the Omega, Sheffield's economic focus has changed from a hub of manufacturing to a medical and university town with an emphasis on health and education. One of the highlights of the year that first saw the light of day in the nineties is still the Twelfth Night surgical ball, a gathering of the city's surgeons. We saw an increase in doctors' and nurses' annual ward parties and retirements, with other medical and GP functions all growing in number. Back in 1982 the only educational function in the diary was Old Edwardians Association from the alumni of King Edward VII School, a group who have been coming every Maundy Thursday since 1982.

The nineties also saw a previously all-American affair arrive on these shores. School Proms appeared, starting with sixth forms and followed in the last two or three years by fifth form events and student graduation balls. The sports and social clubs from manufacturing firms would now appear to have been replaced by functions for accountants, architects and solicitors, which have now grown to the same levels of business that manufacturing-based functions used to generate.

Weddings and Anniversaries

Weddings were always big business for us. By the mid-eighties we had obviously won the trust of our clients to host such an important do. The whole picture has changed since the new law which allowed any establishment to apply for a wedding licence to hold ceremonies. We chose not to apply for a licence as we are party people and not ceremony organisers. The weddings we have now are still traditional. The couple marry in church or the town hall or sometimes another registered venue, then come to us for the party.

It gives us a special pleasure to see a lot of the weddings we do nowadays are for ex-staff, or even the sons and daughters of those who had their wedding reception with us in the eighties. In fact we do more anniversaries than weddings. And there's a nice symmetry when couples who had their wedding at Baldwin's are returning for their 25th wedding anniversary celebrations. To mark such an occasion, we often reproduce the original menu, perhaps updating it with a modern twist.

Birthdays

Birthday parties are an evergreen favourite. The year 1991 was notable for two things. For some reason it was a bumper year for 21st birthday celebrations. But one turned out to be a rather raucous group, whose antics nearly made us reconsider catering for that generation. You know who you are boys!

Function Menus

It is with the private functions that we really get to push out the boundaries with our menus. We can really take the time, planning the best menu for the client and we're always out to impress. It's always possible to improve a dish every time it's served, making a slight adjustment here and there as we strive for perfection. One day perhaps we'll get there.

Here are a few of my special favourites from very recent functions fit for any celebration – even my 70th!

Duck In A Glass

This great dish was unashamedly borrowed from my friend Nigel Haworth of Northcote Manor, Lancashire. This was one of the dishes that pushed him through to the final of BBC2's Great British Menu competition in 2009. Derservedly so, as it's a touch of brilliance!

Ingredients

4 duck legs

1 onion, chopped

6 slices of orange

1 sprig of sage

2 cloves of garlic

500ml red wine

250g duck fat

Half litre of duck stock (frozen, and then defrosted in muslin cloth suspended over a bowl in the fridge)

1 and a half sheets of gelatine

200ml of port, boiled to reduce by half

2 and a half tablespoons redcurrant jelly

For the broad bean purée:

Half an onion, finely chopped

1 clove garlic

100ml double cream

400g broad beans, blanched

100g washed fresh spinach

100ml white wine

250g salted butter

250g duck livers

3 whole eggs

Half a teaspoon salt

Half a teaspoon white pepper

50ml brandy

2 duck breasts

Method

1. To make the liver parfait, melt the butter and heat the brandy. In a food processor blend the livers, eggs, salt and pepper then add the butter and brandy. Pass the mixture through a sieve and into a loaf tin. Sit the loaf tin in a tray of water and place in the oven at 140°c for 30 minutes or until firm. Place in the fridge when cool and chill for 2 hours.

2. For the duck confit, place the chopped onion in the bottom of a tall-sided tray and lay the duck legs on top. Place the orange slices, garlic, sage, red wine and duck fat in the tray, season with salt and pepper and cover with tin foil. Place in the oven at 120°c for 2 hours or until meat is falling from the bone. When cooked leave to cool at room temperature and remove the meat from the bones.

3. For the first layer of the duck glass, take the duck stock and warm in a pan. In a bowl, soak the gelatine sheets in cold water until soft, squeeze out excess water and add to the duck stock. When dissolved split half the duck stock between the glasses and place them in the fridge overnight until set.

4. For the second layer, take the remaining duck stock and combine it with the redcurrant jelly and port reduction. Divide the duck leg meat between the glasses then pour redcurrant duck jelly through a sieve onto the first layer. Place the glasses into the fridge and allow to set.

5. For the third layer, take the liver parfait and cut off any crust formed around the outside, place in a blender and turn on until smooth. Put the mixture in a piping bag, and pipe into the glasses on top of the second layer of leg meat and jelly, and return glasses to the fridge.

6. For the fourth layer, sweat the onion and garlic in a splash of olive oil, add the white wine and reduce by half. Add the double cream and broad beans and simmer for 4-5 minutes. Add the spinach and blend until smooth. Season with salt and pepper and press through a sieve. Allow cooling to room temperature and pour on top of the liver parfait in the glass and return them to the fridge to chill.

7. Finally, take the duck breasts and pull the skin from the meat. Take the skinless breast and sear in a pan and put in an oven at 180°c for 9 minutes. When cooked allow to rest for a further 10 minutes. Take the skin and slice into strips, and then deep fry until crispy.

8. To serve, sprinkle the skin on top of the glass with a slice of duck breast. Serve with buttered croutons.

Chef's Mushroom Ravioli with Sage Butter

You only have to look at the photographs to see that for Stephen this is a labour of love. The dish is all hand-prepared whether it is a table for four in the luncheon restaurant or indeed for 250 as an entrée at a banquet.

Ingredients

For the pasta:

2 whole large eggs

10 egg yolks

150g '00' flour

350g semolina flour

For the filling:

500g chestnut mushrooms, sliced

1 onion, finely diced

2 cloves garlic, finely chopped

1 tablespoon white truffle oil

75g grated Parmesan (plus extra for serving)

2 egg yolks

Salt and pepper

150g salted butter

15 small sage leaves

Method

1. To make the pasta, place all the ingredients in a food processor and blend until forming small balls.

2. Remove from the blender and knead until one large smooth ball.

3. Cover with cling film and allow to rest in the fridge for one hour.

4. In a hot pan fry the mushrooms until just soft and transfer to a bowl. Set aside. In the same pan, fry the onions and garlic gently over a low heat until soft, add the truffle oil and add to the mushrooms and allow to cool.

5. Place the mushroom mix in a blender along with the egg yolks and Parmesan and blend for a few seconds to a coarse consistency. Season to taste and set aside ready to fill the pasta.

6. Using a pasta machine, roll out the pasta into thin sheets and lay on a lightly-floured surface. Cut discs 2cm in diameter and lightly brush with a little egg and water mix.

7. Place a teaspoon of mushroom filling onto each disc and fold over, making sure no air is trapped inside and press together open sides of the ravioli; repeat for 3 to 5 pieces per person, ready to cook.

8. In a separate pan place the butter, and heat until starting to foam. Add the sage leaves and fry until browned.

9. Place the ravioli in a pan of boiling water and cook for 1 minute. Remove from the boiling water and drop into the sage butter, frying for 30 seconds. The ravioli are now ready to serve, topped with extra Parmesan.

Baldwin's Trio of Lamb

This is my favourite way of serving roast lamb. Sometimes we add a fourth element, pan-fried sweetbreads. It is important not to forget the redcurrant jelly accompaniment and please, please, only use fresh homemade mint sauce as indeed do we.

Ingredients

2 French-trimmed racks of lamb

450g lambs' kidneys

1 small shoulder joint of lamb, boned and tied

300ml lamb gravy

2 tomatoes, skinned and diced

60ml double cream

25ml sherry

Method

1. Sear the rack of lamb in hot oil until browned all over.
2. Slice the kidneys in half and remove veins.
3. Lightly rub oil over the outside of the shoulder joint. Season with salt and fresh rosemary, then place in a preheated oven at 160°c for 1 hour 30 minutes.
4. Sprinkle the rack of lamb with sea salt.
5. With 30 minutes to go put the rack of lamb in the oven.
6. When the meat is cooked, rest for 15 minutes. While it is doing so, sauté the kidneys in a frying pan and finish with diced tomatoes, double cream and a little sherry.
7. Slice a piece of shoulder joint, two pieces of the rack of lamb, bone showing and serve on a warm plate with a spoonful of kidneys.
8. Serve with the vegetables in season and homemade lamb gravy, redcurrant jelly and mint sauce.

Chef's Stem Ginger Ice Cream

This is a great Ice cream, particularly served with rhubarb dishes, although the majority of our desserts are served with homemade ice cream.

Ingredients

13 egg yolks

200g caster sugar

400g glucose

1150 ml double cream

6 balls of stem ginger, diced

You will need an ice cream maker

Method

1. Put the cream and glucose in a thick bottomed pan and bring to the boil.
2. Whisk the egg yolks and sugar together then add the hot cream. Place back in the pan and thicken over a low heat. Do not allow to boil.
3. When thick, put the diced stem ginger into the mixture and leave in a fridge to cool.
4. Pour into the ice cream maker and churn for 50 minutes, then remove. Seal in an airtight tub and freeze.

Funerals

We've had lots of funerals. Inevitably, some of them have been the funerals of close friends; here are just three happy sad memories.

Marti Caine

Marti Caine was known to many of us in Sheffield as Our Lynn. About a week before she died following a long and courageous fight against cancer, she sent a friend to see me with her own instructions for the programme of music for her funeral, which was of course attended by all her Sheffield friends and many of the showbiz glitterati. Amongst many things, Marti was famous for her Snow White pantomimes and she'd asked the pianist Colin 'fingers' Henry to play songs from the show. As he started to play, pantomime dwarves appeared on to the dance floor and started to do the march. Within 5 minutes many of the congregation in the room joined in, shuffling along on their knees singing 'Hi ho, hi ho, it's off to work we go'. It was a very poignant and memorable moment, a fitting tribute to a wonderful lady.

Jim Hawkins

Jim Hawkins, a great friend and rare character and above all a damn fine caterer. For many years he ran Whitley Hall and Aston Hall with his wife Angela and in later years ran the fine catering at Bramall Lane. He died after a long illness but he never lost his zest for life or his sense of humour. The funeral lunch was a hive of funny Hawkins stories. The family were welcomed to the Omega after the internment by music from Dave Brennan and the Stomper New Orleans Parade Band. A fantastic afternoon, and a marvellous celebration of the man.

Keith Healey

The funeral of Keith Healey (alias Jason King), a famous bon viveur of the city, drew many mourners. I had the honour of giving a eulogy which was preceded by his masonic friends and I decided to tell a few of the old stories. I congratulated Marge on getting him out on time fully dressed and made up by noon and recalled the story of his white Rolls-Royce. Keith arrived in the snow one January and got it stuck in the car park. At the approach of the wedding season in March the phone rang. "Have you seen my Rolls? I can't remember where I've left it. I think I last saw it at your place in the snow and I have a wedding at the weekend". Generously, I didn't charge him for long-stay parking. They don't make them like Jason any more.

Recipe for festive treats

IF you've had a staff Christmas party this year, chances are it will have been at Baldwin's Omega, which serves up around 10,000 turkey dinners.

Boss David Baldwin's thyme and walnut stuffing is justly famous.

When Food & Drink published the recipe a couple of years back it was a great success, so here it is again.

You need: 12oz wholemeal breadcrumbs; 6oz finely chopped onion; 2 medium carrots, grated; 6oz shelled walnuts; 2oz chopped parsley; juice and grated rind of a lemon; 4 eggs; 1teaspoon salt; tablespoons walnut oil;

4 heaped tablespoons dried thyme (or two fresh); oil to fry

Heat the oil in a saucepan and cook carrot and onion until soft. Add hebs and nuts and cook on for five minutes.

Add rind, salt and crumbs and cook, stirrng continually, for another two. Remove from heat, add beaten eggs to bind, with a little hot water if needed.

Shape into two-inch wide discs, half an inch thick.

Place on a greased baking try, lightly brushing with walnut oil. Bake for 15 minutes at gas mark 5 (375F, 190C) while turkey is resting.

Our highly acclaimed thyme and walnut stuffing has always been a big hit
Reproduced with kind permission from Sheffield Newspapers Ltd.

Christmas

We love Christmas at Baldwin's. As might be expected, it is our major trading period and a very special time of year. Pauline spends a great deal of time decorating our rooms and the tables each night. Throughout December we do Christmas party nights made up of many small parties.

The night starts at 7.30 with a glass of bubbly followed by a five-course Christmas party menu. Apart from the turkey, each year chef and I spend a long time carefully considering a menu to ring the changes. Our aim is to make full use of seasonal produce, and it goes without saying that our principle of making everything from scratch applies equally at this time of year. The kitchens are flat out making over 1500 mince pies a week, all made freshly on the day they will be served. Our chefs also make our own festive chocolates as well as our own breads. It's also important to serve up a really good vegetarian dish for those who choose not to eat meat, in order to give them the Christmas feeling. Each night our Christmas puddings are presented by our very own Santa whose identity is secret. Of course you and I know he's the real one, but keep it quiet. The service ends with a spectacular show when we flame the puddings in the room.

Give your turkey the RIGHT STUFF

By Martin Dawes
FOOD WRITER

NOBODY cooks more turkey dinners than big David Baldwin. He will serve up over 4,000 of them at his Omega banqueting suite on Psalter Lane, Sheffield, this Christmas.

So he knows about stuffing. His thyme and walnut stuffing, based on an old recipe, is a firm favourite.

David serves it as small round discs baked for 15 minutes. He strongly advises people not to stuff their birds because cooking times need to be longer to avoid the risk of salmonella.

"You'll get the same effect by seasoning the inside of the bird, adding an onion and the herb you are using, in this case thyme," he says.

The secret ingredient is carrot, which adds sweetness to the stuffing.

What you need for ten people:

12oz wholewheat breadcrumbs
6oz finely chopped onion
2 medium grated carrots
6oz shelled walnuts
2oz chopped parsley
Juice and grated rind of one lemon
4 eggs

Method:

Heat oil in saucepan over medium heat. Add carrot and onion and cook until soft, then add herbs and nuts and cook on for five minutes. Add rind, seasoning and breadcrumbs and cook, stirring continuously, for two minutes

Remove from heat, add beaten eggs and bind, using a little hot weater if needed.

Shape into discs two inches in diameter and half an inch thick. Place on greased baking try, lightly brush stuffing with walnut oil and bake for 15 minutes at gas mark 5 (375F, 190C)

■ David's tip: With big turkeys loosen or cut off legs (cooked separately) to ensure even cooking.

The Perfect Turkey

Christmas always means turkey, that's what the customers want so we spend time, along with our butcher, sourcing the best for our table. Having found the best, it follows that cooking it should be done with great care. It's so easy to get something so simple so horribly wrong. Turkey is the only meat we can't carve in the room as we can't do it fast enough to keep everything hot. So it is important right at the start to find a succulent bird that won't become dry. This year our butcher Jimmy has introduced us to the Grove Smith family farm near Braintree. They have a plough to plate philosophy of care for their birds that produces the finest quality meat. I'm enthusiastic about supporting British farmers but the turkey industry is one we need to be careful with as there is immense pressure on these farmers to produce cheaper meat for the fast food industry and supermarkets, especially at Christmas. Grove Smith has been in the business of producing quality turkey for over 40 Years. They neither deal with the bigger supermarkets nor compromise on their techniques. Being arable farmers, they maintain an organic cycle of producing their own food for the turkeys and the turkeys produce the fertilisers for the land that feeds the food that feeds them. The turkeys are all bred in-house. They are even processed on site to avoid any unnecessary stress to the birds. As I hear so often keeping them clean and calm with a lot of sunlight and good quality food produces the best meat. Grove Smith have developed their own feeding regime that encourages the birds to retain fat as it is the fat that is the key to succulent moist meat, which is not always easy to create.

We have been holding Christmas party nights from the beginning and as with our other occasions have been given great support by Sheffield Newspapers and my friend Martin Dawes, who always wants to know my verdict on turkey.

```
      NEW YEAR'S EVE AT BALDWIN'S OMEGA, 1981
      7.00 p.m. to 7.30 p.m. - Champagne Reception
                    ********
                     Menu

             Ogen Melon Surprise
                   ********

                Soup Baldwin
                 **********

            Tay Salmon en cocotte
                  *********

               Sorbet 81/82
                 *********

          Fillet of Beef Napoleon
       Pommes Parisienne, Petit Pois
           Florets of Cauliflour
                 *********

                Cognac cones
                 *********

          Cheese Board and celery
                 *********

          Petit Fours and Coffee
                 *********
```

New Year's Eve

New Year's Eve is the biggest night in the social calendar. For many years, it was our main event – until our New Year's Eve Ball became too popular. We have a limit on capacity dictated by fire regulations, which meant that New Year's Eve always sold out, forcing us to turn away good clients who came to all sorts of events during the rest of the year.

It became a customer relations nightmare so we stopped doing New Year altogether until the new millennium. We didn't open on the evening of the millennium but on 31st January we put back the Christmas decorations and had guests welcomed by a piper and recreated New Year for all of those who had missed it the first time.

Among the 250 celebrating that evening, were essential workers and some people who had been ill in hospital at the time of the original celebrations. By midnight when we counted down the New Year and sang Auld Lang Syne, the clients got into the spirit as if it was the real thing and the champagne orders were flooding in. It was one of our most memorable spoofs. Our cabaret, Dave Berry, helped make it very special.

Christmas Greetings

-Baldwin's Omega-

-Pauline Shearstone-

Ω Baldwin's Omega

Best Wishes for

Christmas and the New Year

from

David & Pauline Baldwin & the staff

Ω Baldwin's Omega

Brincliffe Hill (off Psalter Lane), Sheffield S11 9DE
Telephone: Sheffield 53263/51818

DAD
AT
WORK

Portrait by Polly - Age 9

The Family Feel

The Family Feel

It is important to Pauline and I that the restaurant always has that personal family-run feel. The business has seen several generations of staff families members pass through the building in different roles. Pam, Mary and Angela's children have all worked in the building at some time and for many years Mary Booker and her son Raymond were a strong team in the kitchen. We are pleased that many of the wedding bookings we have taken in recent years have been from old staff members. It is always good to see everyone return to the building for their own family celebrations.

All of our children have all been involved at different times, Ben as pot washer and bar service, while Polly has tried her hand at most roles in the building from potato peeler to layup staff, florist and bar services. David has helped with the refurbishment of both the bars and our famous toilets. Although they are not directly involved now they all still have a passion for the restaurant and fond memories of both working and celebrating family functions here.

Baldwin's and me

I was once asked if Baldwin's Omega and my parents business has affected me. After a long pause I replied 'In a lot of ways it's made me who I am today'. To be as successful as my folks you have to live and breathe your business and in our case we ate it too.

I can't eat out in a restaurant without lifting the plate upside down to see who made the china or have a gin and tonic unless it is from a freshly opened bottle of tonic and really good gin. I check out the toilets in every restaurant I eat in and when dining out I always sit facing the restaurant so I can watch the service. I can't get through a meal without tasting everybody else's on the table and of course you can never order the same thing as anyone else. I can probably tell you what I had in each restaurant I have eaten in with my parents since I was 6 and there are a lot. One day I will write my own book on 'a lifetime of eating out with Mr and Mrs B'. When out to dinner as a family we all fight to sit furthest away from dad and we are fast eaters. The danger of savouring your meal and taking your time is that dad might eat it before you, every meal is a learning experience.

So yes you can definitely say my parents and their business has moulded me as a person. I feel extremely lucky to have eaten in some of the finest restaurants and stayed in some fantastic hotels, all in the name of research and of course my parents enthusiasm for pleasure.

I am immensely proud of my parents, they are a tough act to follow. Baldwin's Omega has always been a huge part of my life, that comes with its ups and downs. Downs such as too much turkey for tea in December so much so that I can't eat any now and ups like my tremendous 21st birthday party and my brother's wedding and who else has their name on their own pink champagne.

Baldwin's is a special place to me and always will be.

Polly Baldwin

I've lost half a finger...
...but gained countless experiences!

When I was asked to write a short passage for this book, it occurred to me that I could probably write a book myself on the things I've got up to in that building. But instead here are a few random thoughts.

I've learned countless things over the years from my mum and dad and like any child of course you take on their morals and values and make them into your own. But as a Baldwin you almost exclusively learn these values in the work place, because that's what we do. We work very hard at whatever it is we do and you'll rarely hear us complain because we love it.

My earliest memory of the Omega was day one. Not sure how old I was but I remember sitting in the front of a huge lorry with all sorts of ovens and kitchen bits on the back. It had all been removed from the Hillsborough Suite ready to be moved to the Omega. I think I'd been left with the lorry driver so I was out from under the feet of everyone else. My next clearest memory was being put to work as a kitchen porter on a Saturday afternoon at the age of around 8 or 9. You'll see a pattern developing here. This was again to get me out from under Mum's feet. It's in that kitchen I lost half a finger (a tendency to exaggerate slightly is another Baldwin trait) when I sliced it off with a potato peeler. Not satisfied with this, the following week I grazed all my knuckles after sticking both hands into the potato rumble while it was still going. Despite my injuries I still hated leaving and used to cry when 4.30 pm came and I was put on the 272 bus home. I worked there all through my A levels and in the summers while at drama school. My parents have worked and continue to work harder than anyone else I know, in truth probably a little too hard. To me Baldwin's Omega is a community. The community they've built together has meant a great deal. More than anything else, it's a living testimony to what they've achieved in business. You only have to look at their staff, the extended Baldwin family who have been with them for years and years. As I now employ my own staff I look to emulate the same mutual respect that exists at the Omega. I'll leave you with these two thoughts. The first is my philosophy, which is strongly influenced by Mr and Mrs B and the second is the greatest piece of advice dad has ever given me.

'Work Hard, Play Hard'

'You only get out of life what you put in'

Ben Baldwin

David Baldwin Jnr on Baldwin's Omega

My earliest memory of the Omega? Now give me a minute, it really was a long time ago. We were holidaying on a narrow boat, thanks to a slight navigational error by Captain Pappa we found ourselves moored under a motorway bridge at Ellesmere Port of all places.

Pauline, always one to make the best of a tricky situation was not fazed by our unlikely holiday location. She secured everything, and I mean everything, that was possibly worth stealing then went ashore. The local hostelry was full of permed hair, tattoos and super glossy shell suits but dad can blend in like a chameleon and we were soon accepted by the locals, swapping rounds and breathing a sigh of relief.

Early the next day we retreated back to Chester under the cover of the early morning industrial smog. No sooner had we moored, dad announced he had to shoot back to Sheffield to complete the legals on an exciting new business deal. All hell was breaking loose back at base, but you would never have known it. Dad's not exactly the iceman, but he can come surprisingly close at times.

And the rest, as they say, is history...

We really have had some great parties at Baldwin's over the years. From our engagement to our wedding, both Angus and Oscar's many birthdays, my 40th and Alex's 40th to name but a few. Each party has been a huge giggle and some even life-changing.

People constantly ask me how my dad can cater for so many people, and yet manage to make every meal as perfect as the next. I reply that it is cooking on an industrial scale... with lots of love.

I would like to charge my glass and toast my dad, true legend in his very own lunchtime.

Bon appetit!

David Jnr

Jonny and the boys at Aigua Blava Hotel, Summer 2010

The art of liberal pouring demonstrated by Jonny. He spent two winters with us at Baldwin's and this was one of the skills we passed on.

Being a junior Baldwin...

Imagine at the age of 6 and 7 not wanting a McDonalds... not even being tempted by the free toy.

"Is there anywhere we can get something like in Aigua Blava?" we would ask. Although my brother and I are now 11 and 12, we realised from an early age that our Grandad's passion for great food had been passed on.

When ordering in a restaurant we love to see the waiters' faces when they double check we want our steaks really rare. We don't know whether our appreciation for good food is nature or nurture, but what we do know, is that we want to continue to learn more about food and look forward to the day when we can join Grandad in the business for our first pocket-money jobs.

Mum reckons that the reason we like our food so much is down to the genes. We're happy with that!

Angus and Oscar Baldwin

The Mr B Recipe *(What maketh the man, by David Baldwin Jr.)*

To make industrial catering with lots of love – Serves 200 people (Do not try this at home)

Ingredients & Method

1 very large man

Yes, he's always been large, big and powerful although has a concealed, soft, gooey centre.

1 good wife

Behind every great man is a woman more talented, more patient and more capable than that man. Although mother would never, ever admit to even a fraction of her skill base or relentless talents.

Several 20kg bags of sporting skills

Divide equally into climbing, water polo, cycling, cricket, tennis and golf.

25l of impatience

Especially when a) tired & b) hungry. (Explosive Warning: Never mix both at the same time).

30l of trust

Will eventually let you do it your way, though it was probably his idea in the first place.

350 quarts of life's zest and laughter

Any time, any place, anywhere but must be very loud.

15 cloves of questionable driving skills

Less said the better... he drives like he's just stolen it.

166 cups of determination, relentless, gut-busting determination

2 large handfuls of sea salt

Oh he does love his holidays. They are the passport to every corner of his gastronomic world.

100 kilos of serious generosity, verging on philanthropy at times.

Rest for 2hrs

Anywhere at all, dinner table, car, sofa, kitchen floor. The undisputed king of cat-napping.

Serve hot and always with a smile.

A Word from our Fellow Directors...

...Friends Indeed

At the dawn of the new decade of the 1980s our family business was enjoying the most prosperous time of its 90 year history and we launched a policy of providing investment to assist other local businesses. It was as a result of this that in early 1981 our solicitors, Keeble Hawson, introduced us to David and Pauline Baldwin with a business plan to acquire the Omega Restaurant and re-open it. David had already established a name for himself in the catering world but the Omega had been languishing badly since its heyday in the 1960s, mostly due to its unwieldy size. The key to the Baldwin's plan, however, was to use the copious space to advantage by converting to banqueting, which they had successfully achieved at Sheffield Wednesday's Hillsborough Suite. We were impressed with the project from the start. Talks began and we agreed to fund the deal for a period of nine months, by which time other funding was to have been in place.

It was explained that a major building company had recently offered £320,000 for the whole site which had planning permission for 13 houses on the eastern part. This put a market value of £120,000 on the building area leaving a value of £200,000 on the restaurant area. Based on this valuation, contracts were exchanged on 29 May 1981 for completion on 28 August.

When the time came it was decided to discard the building plot, which would only be a distraction from the main focus and unnecessary for the business. Everything is easier in retrospect and this turned out to be a big mistake. As a result of ensuing circumstances, rear access to the restaurant was at first limited and then cut off. Deliveries became difficult and fire engine access was virtually impossible. Licence renewal would be unlikely.

If the Omega was to have a chance of success there was no option but for Turner's to buy the building plot to sort out the mess. We were then able to restore the access, reduce the plot to retain the lawn area to the east of the restaurant and sell the project on to a reputable local builder. Our permanent right of way was protected in the process.

All of this did no good to the business and its funding sources. A restructure became urgently essential. In March 1982 Hillsborough Suite Limited gave way to Baldwin's Omega Limited, with Don Lyon and myself joining David and Pauline on the board of directors. With all the acquisition and financing problems eventually resolved, the focus could now be directed on creating the business. Needless to say, over the next 30 years the outcome has been there for all to see – and more importantly to enjoy.

There is no doubt at all that it was well worth weathering those initial storms. Thanks to David, Pauline, their long serving core team and a lot of dedication and hard work, Sheffield is proud of a banqueting facility which is second to none.

On a final personal note I must say it has given me a huge amount of pleasure and satisfaction to have played a part and is an honour to remain as chairman.

Ashley Turner